Taste of Home
CAST IRON
COOKBOOK

TASTE OF HOME BOOKS • RDA ENTHUSIAST BRANDS, LLC • MILWAUKEE, WI

© 2021 RDA Enthusiast Brands, LLC.
1610 N. 2nd St., Suite 102, Milwaukee, WI 53212-3906
All rights reserved. Taste of Home is a registered
trademark of RDA Enthusiast Brands, LLC.

Visit us at **tasteofhome.com** for other Taste of Home
books and products.

International Standard Book Number:
978-1-62145-714-5
Library of Congress Control Number: 2020949316
Component Number:
116700104H

Executive Editor: Mark Hagen
Senior Art Director: Raeann Thompson
Assistant Art Director: Courtney Lovetere
Designer: Jazmin Delgado
Deputy Editor, Copy Desk: Dulcie Shoener
Copy Editor: Ann Walter

Cover
Photographer: Mark Derse
Set Stylist: Melissa Franco
Food Stylist: Shannon Norris

Pictured on front cover:
Parmesan-Bacon Bubble Bread, p. 36

Pictured on back cover:
Greek Tilapia, p. 86
Zippy Turkey Zoodles, p. 61
Classic Sweet Potato Pie, p. 105

Printed in USA
1 3 5 7 9 10 8 6 4 2

P. 53

P. 60

P. 80

P. 20

There's no doubt about it—cast-iron skillets are lifesavers for today's home cooks. From seared steaks and tender chicken to golden cornbread and deep-dish pizzas, all-time family favorites come together in a snap with a cast-iron skillet.

Now, the team at *Taste of Home* offers a brand-new collection, **Cast Iron Cooking,** which includes all of the dishes your gang craves. Sizzling steaks that are cooked to perfection, roasted vegetables that make eating healthy a snap, and crisps, cobblers and other sweets that come together easily in a skillet.

No cast iron? No worry! You'll still be able to use this exciting new book. Grab your favorite skillet and take advantage of all the fantastic stovetop staples offered here. Similarly, any ovenproof skillet allows you to enjoy each of the baked bites inside this red-hot collection.

You'll enjoy...

- 135 must-try entrees, sides, breakfasts and more made in a skillet

- 🄳 A 5-Ingredient icon highlighting recipes that call for just a handful of ingredients (not including water, salt, pepper, oils or optional items)

- 🕑 A Fast Fix icon spotlighting dishes that are ready in just half an hour or less

- Appetizers and snacks perfect for parties and special occasions as well as cozy movie nights at home with the family

- Crisps, cobblers, grunts and other sweets made easily in a skillet

From cast-iron greats to weeknight timesavers, the recipes in **Taste of Home Cast Iron Cooking** turn out smokin' hot and deliciously delightful each and every time!

More ways to connect with us: f 🐦 📷 📌

SHOPTASTEOFHOME.COM

CONTENTS

P. 44

P. 13

A CRASH COURSE IN **CAST IRON**

Durable and versatile, the cast-iron skillet is a true kitchen workhorse that will last a lifetime and cook almost anything—from breakfast to one-dish dinners to delicious desserts. Whether your skillet is new, a family heirloom or a flea market find, take some time to learn how to treat it right, then get started with the recipes in this book!

HOW TO SEASON A CAST-IRON SKILLET

Clean. Scrub with hot water and a stiff brush to remove any rust.

Oil. Drop a tablespoon of vegetable oil on the pan; spread it around with a paper towel. Oil the entire outside of the skillet, including the handle. Wipe off excess oil with a folded paper towel. The skillet should be just lightly greased.

Heat. Set the oven to 350°; put a piece of foil on the bottom rack. Place the skillet, face down, on the upper rack for about an hour, letting it heat up with the oven. Turn the oven off; leave the pan inside until it's cool. The oil bakes into the pores of the pan, creating a nonstick finish.

Repeat. Oil up the skillet and heat it all over again for an almost glassy surface of seasoning.

HOW TO SAVE A RUSTY SKILLET

Scour. Get the pan wet, add a little dish soap, then scrub with a piece of steel wool or a tough scrubber. Scrub in small circles, focusing on the rusted areas first. Scrub until you see the original black iron emerge, then rinse.

Scrub with a sponge. To make sure the skillet is clean, scrub again—this time with a soapy sponge. Buff off any residue or rusty bits that remain.

Dry. Use a clean dishrag to dry the skillet. Don't use a rag you're fond of; the iron can leave dark stains. To dry it completely, place skillet on the stove and turn on the heat for a couple of minutes.

For small jobs: For a pan that has small amounts of rust but doesn't need a complete scouring, simply dampen a paper towel with oil and use it to wipe away the rust.

HOW TO CARE FOR CAST IRON

- **DO** clean immediately after use (after the pan cools).

- **DO** wait until the pan is cool to the touch before washing it in the sink. Submerging hot cast iron in cold water can cause it to crack.

- **DO** use hot water and soap. It's a common misconception that soap will strip the seasoning from cast iron—it's OK to go ahead and suds up.

- **DON'T** let it soak too long. Cast iron + extended exposure to water = rust.

TYPES OF
HEAVY METAL

The two most common types of cast iron are traditional bare cast iron and enameled cast iron. They behave similarly, but there are some notable differences. Here's the rundown to help you master cast-iron cooking.

ENAMELED CAST IRON
PROS
- Available in a variety of attractive colors
- Can cook acidic ingredients without harming surface
- Does not retain flavors of foods after using

CONS
- Can be expensive
- Not as durable as traditional cast iron; enamel coating can chip if mishandled
- Food more likely to stick than on traditional cast iron
- Takes longer to heat up than traditional cast iron

TRADITIONAL CAST IRON
PROS
- Inexpensive
- Can be used over an open flame, such as a grill or campfire
- Practically indestructible and will last a lifetime (maybe longer!) if properly seasoned and cared for
- Foods are not very likely to stick if the cast iron is properly seasoned

CONS
- Prone to rust; needs to be seasoned every once in a while
- Not practical for all foods; tomatoes and other acidic ingredients will cause seasoning to wear off
- May retain flavors of foods, such as fried fish, after using

FOCACCIA BARESE, PAGE 12

CAST IRON
SNACKS & STARTERS

Need an extra special appetizer or savory snack for a casual get-together? Put your cast-iron skillet to good use when cooking up a mouthwatering party pleaser.

READY IN 30 MINS.

SKILLET NACHOS

MANDARIN CHICKEN BITES

Instead of a big Christmas meal, our family enjoys nibbling on an all-day appetizer buffet. Each year we present tempting new dishes alongside our favorites. This is one of those tried-and-true dishes that's a must.
—*Susannah Yinger, Canal Winchester, OH*

Takes: 30 min. • **Makes:** 15 servings

    1   cup all-purpose flour
    ½   tsp. salt
    ¼   tsp. pepper
    1   lb. boneless skinless chicken breasts,
        cut into 2-in. cubes
    2   Tbsp. butter
    1   can (11 oz.) mandarin oranges,
        drained
    ⅔   cup orange marmalade
    ½   tsp. dried tarragon

1. In a large bowl, combine the flour, salt and pepper. Add chicken, a few pieces at a time, and turn to coat.
2. In a skillet, brown chicken in butter until no longer pink. In a small saucepan, combine the oranges, marmalade and tarragon; bring to a boil. Pour over chicken; stir gently to coat. Serve warm, with toothpicks.
1 piece: 124 cal., 2g fat (1g sat. fat), 21mg chol., 115mg sod., 19g carb. (12g sugars, 0 fiber), 7g pro.

"Although we have a few old favorites that we look forward to each year, I went looking for a new appetizer to serve at my family's Christmas Eve get-together. Since we always attend church on the evening of Christmas Eve, I need items that I can either prepare ahead of time that need just a little warm-up, or that can go together quickly, so there is little to do when we return home. This recipe fit perfectly—it was quick, easy and absolutely delicious."
BECKY66, TASTEOFHOME.COM

SKILLET NACHOS

My mom gave me a fundraiser cookbook, and my favorite and most used recipe is one for skillet nachos. My family loves it, too. For toppings, try sour cream, tomatoes, jalapeno and red onion.
—*Judy Hughes, Waverly, KS*

Takes: 30 min. • **Makes:** 6 servings

    1   lb. ground beef
    1   can (14½ oz.) diced tomatoes,
        undrained
    1   cup fresh or frozen corn, thawed
    ¾   cup uncooked instant rice
    ½   cup water
    1   envelope taco seasoning
    ½   tsp. salt
    1   cup shredded Colby-Monterey
        Jack cheese
    1   pkg. (16 oz.) tortilla chips

Optional toppings: Sour cream, sliced fresh jalapenos, shredded lettuce and lime wedges

1. In a large skillet, cook beef over medium heat until it is no longer pink, 6-8 minutes, breaking into crumbles; drain. Stir in the tomatoes, corn, rice, water, taco seasoning and salt. Bring to a boil. Reduce the heat; simmer, covered, until rice is tender and mixture is slightly thickened, 8-10 minutes.
2. Remove from heat; sprinkle with cheese. Let stand, covered, until cheese is melted, about 5 minutes. Divide tortilla chips among 6 plates; spoon beef mixture over chips. Serve with toppings as desired.
1 serving: 676 cal., 31g fat (10g sat. fat), 63mg chol., 1293mg sod., 74g carb. (4g sugars, 4g fiber), 25g pro.

MANDARIN
CHICKEN BITES

QUESO FUNDIDO

Dig in to this hot one-skillet dip and savor the gooey cheese and spicy kick from chorizo and pepper jack.
—*Julie Merriman, Seattle, WA*

- -

Prep: 20 min. • **Bake:** 15 min. • **Makes:** 6 cups

- 1 lb. uncooked chorizo
- 2 cups fresh or frozen corn, thawed
- 1 large red onion, chopped
- 1 poblano pepper, chopped
- 8 oz. fresh goat cheese, crumbled
- 2 cups cubed Monterey Jack cheese
- 1 cup cubed pepper jack cheese
- 1 large tomato, seeded and chopped
- 3 green onions, thinly sliced
  Blue corn tortilla chips

1. Preheat oven to 350°. Crumble chorizo into a 10-in. cast-iron or other ovenproof skillet; add corn, red onion and pepper. Cook over medium heat until meat is fully cooked, 6-8 minutes; drain. Stir in the cheeses.
2. Bake until bubbly, 14-16 minutes. Sprinkle with tomato and green onions. Serve dip with chips.
¼ cup: 161 cal., 12g fat (6g sat. fat), 38mg chol., 365mg sod., 4g carb. (1g sugars, 1g fiber), 9g pro.

FRIED ASPARAGUS

This beer-battered deep-fried asparagus is a favorite at events. For even more flavor, dip pieces into cool ranch dressing.
—*Lori Kimble, Montgomery, AL*

- -

Takes: 30 min. • **Makes:** 2½ dozen

- 1 cup all-purpose flour
- ¾ cup cornstarch
- 1¼ tsp. salt
- 1¼ tsp. baking powder
- ¾ tsp. baking soda
- ¾ tsp. garlic salt
- ½ tsp. pepper
- 1 cup beer or nonalcoholic beer
- 3 large egg whites
- 2½ lbs. fresh asparagus, trimmed
  Oil for deep-fat frying
  Ranch salad dressing

1. In a bowl, combine the first 7 ingredients. Combine beer and egg whites; stir into the dry ingredients just until moistened. Dip asparagus into batter.
2. In a deep cast-iron or electric skillet, heat 1½ in. oil to 375°. Fry asparagus in batches until golden brown, 2-3 minutes on each side. Remove from skillet and drain on paper towels. Serve asparagus immediately with ranch salad dressing.
1 piece: 70 cal., 4g fat (0 sat. fat), 0 chol., 207mg sod., 7g carb. (1g sugars, 0 fiber), 1g pro.

QUESO FUNDIDO

MARINATED SHRIMP

My husband's aunt shared this appetizer recipe with me ages ago. Not only is it a Christmas Eve tradition in our home, but in the homes of our grown children as well.
—*Delores Hill, Helena, MT*

Prep: 10 min. + marinating • **Cook:** 10 min.
Makes: about 3 dozen

- 2 lbs. uncooked jumbo shrimp, peeled and deveined
- 1 cup olive oil
- 2 garlic cloves, minced
- 4 tsp. dried rosemary, crushed
- 2 tsp. dried oregano
- 2 bay leaves
- 1 cup dry white wine or chicken broth
- ¾ tsp. salt
- ⅛ tsp. pepper

1. In a bowl, combine the shrimp, oil, garlic, rosemary, oregano and bay leaves. Cover and refrigerate for 2-4 hours.
2. Pour shrimp and marinade into a large deep skillet. Add wine or broth, salt and pepper. Cover and cook over medium-low heat for 10-15 minutes or until shrimp turn pink, stirring occasionally. Discard bay leaves. Transfer shrimp with a slotted spoon to a serving dish.
1 piece: 40 cal., 2g fat (0 sat. fat), 31mg chol., 42mg sod., 0 carb. (0 sugars, 0 fiber), 4g pro.

MUFFULETTA WELLINGTONS

MUFFULETTA WELLINGTONS

These fun snack-sized sandwiches were inspired by the muffuletta, a layered deli meat and olive salad sandwich originating in New Orleans. They have all the goodness of a classic muffuletta baked inside convenient refrigerated pizza dough. Feel free to swap the ham or salami for turkey or roast beef.
—*Chelsea Madren, Fullerton, CA*

Prep: 25 min. • **Bake:** 20 min. + standing
Makes: 6 servings

- 3 Tbsp. melted butter, divided
- 1 Tbsp. cornmeal
- 1 tube (13.8 oz.) refrigerated pizza crust
- 6 Tbsp. olive bruschetta
- 18 slices thinly sliced hard salami
- 12 slices thinly sliced Black Forest deli ham
- 6 slices part-skim mozzarella cheese
- 6 slices provolone cheese
- 1 Tbsp. sesame seeds

Preheat oven to 425°. Grease a 12-in. cast-iron or other ovenproof skillet with 1 Tbsp. butter. Sprinkle with cornmeal; set aside. Unroll the pizza dough; cut into 6 portions. On a floured surface, roll each portion into a 6-in. square. Place 1 Tbsp. olive salad in center of each square; top with salami, ham, mozzarella cheese and provolone cheese. Bring 4 corners of dough together above filling; pinch the edges to seal. Place in prepared skillet, seam side down. Brush with remaining 2 Tbsp. butter; sprinkle with the sesame seeds. Bake until golden brown, 20-25 minutes. Let stand for 10 minutes before serving.
1 sandwich: 562 cal., 33g fat (14g sat. fat), 93mg chol., 1815mg sod., 37g carb. (6g sugars, 1g fiber), 32g pro.

FOCACCIA BARESE

This focaccia recipe has been in my mom's family for several generations. It is one of my most-requested baked items whenever I'm invited to a party or potluck—I'm not allowed to attend unless I bring it!
—*Dora Travaglio, Mount Prospect, IL*

- -

Prep: 30 min. + rising • **Bake:** 30 min.
Makes: 8 servings

- 1⅛ tsp. active dry yeast
- ¾ cup warm water
  (110° to 115°), divided
- ½ tsp. sugar
- ⅓ cup mashed potato flakes
- 1½ tsp. plus 2 Tbsp. olive oil, divided
- ¼ tsp. salt
- 1¾ cups bread flour

TOPPING
- 2 medium tomatoes, thinly sliced
- ¼ cup pitted Greek olives, halved
- 1½ tsp. minced fresh or dried oregano
- ½ tsp. coarse salt

1. In a large bowl, dissolve yeast in ½ cup warm water. Add the sugar; let stand for 5 minutes. Add the potato flakes, 1½ tsp. oil, salt, 1 cup flour and remaining water. Beat until smooth. Stir in enough remaining flour to form a soft dough.
2. Turn onto a floured surface; knead until smooth and elastic, 6-8 minutes. Place in a greased bowl, turning once to grease the top. Cover and let rise in a warm place until doubled, about 1 hour. Punch dough down. Cover and let rest for 10 minutes.
3. Place 1 Tbsp. olive oil in a 10-in. cast-iron or other ovenproof skillet; tilt pan to evenly coat. Add dough; shape to fit pan. Cover and let rise until doubled, about 30 minutes.
4. With fingertips, make several dimples over top of dough. Brush with remaining 1 Tbsp. of oil. Blot tomato slices with paper towels. Arrange tomato slices and olives over dough; sprinkle with oregano and salt.
5. Bake at 375° for 30-35 minutes or until golden brown.
1 slice: 142 cal., 4g fat (0 sat. fat), 0 chol., 269mg sod., 24g carb. (1g sugars, 1g fiber), 4g pro. **Diabetic exchanges:** 1½ starch, ½ fat.

KHRUSTYKY

I honor my Ukrainian heritage by serving khrustyky—a crispy, dainty pastry dusted with confectioners' sugar—on Christmas Eve as part of the traditional feast of 12 dishes. Each dish symbolizes one of the 12 apostles. This sweet treat has an eggy flavor similar to cream puffs.
—*Carol Funk, Richard, SK*

- -

Prep: 25 min. • **Cook:** 20 min.
Makes: 1½ dozen pastries

- 2 large eggs, room temperature
- 3 large egg yolks, room temperature
- 1 Tbsp. heavy whipping cream
- 1 Tbsp. vanilla extract
- 2 Tbsp. sugar
- 1½ cups all-purpose flour
- ½ tsp. salt
  Oil for deep-fat frying
  Confectioners' sugar

1. In a large bowl, beat the eggs, egg yolks, cream and vanilla. Beat in sugar. Combine flour and salt; stir into the egg mixture just until smooth (dough will be soft). Divide into 4 portions.
2. On a well-floured surface, roll out 1 dough portion to ⅛-in. thickness. Cut into 1½-in. strips; cut strips diagonally into 3 pieces. Cut a 1½-in. slit lengthwise into the center of each piece; pull 1 end of strip through slit to make a loop. Cover shaped pieces while rolling out and cutting the remaining dough.
3. In a deep cast-iron or electric skillet, heat 2-3 in. of oil to 375°. Fry pastries, in batches, until golden brown, turning once. Remove from skillet and drain on paper towels. Dust with confectioners' sugar.
1 pastry: 83 cal., 4g fat (1g sat. fat), 52mg chol., 75mg sod., 10g carb. (2g sugars, 0 fiber), 2g pro.

PEPPERONI
FOCACCIA BREAD

PEPPERONI FOCACCIA BREAD

This focaccia bread is perfect to include as part of a pasta dinner, either as an appetizer or sliced for sandwiches. You will love the aroma while it bakes—it's hard to wait for it to be done! I add thinly sliced plum tomatoes and fresh basil on top.
—*Trisha Kruse, Eagle, ID*

Prep: 25 min. • **Bake:** 20 min. + cooling
Makes: 8 servings

- 1 pkg. (3½ oz.) sliced pepperoni, chopped
- ½ medium onion, thinly sliced
- 1 large egg, room temperature
- 1 cup 2% milk
- ½ cup plain Greek yogurt
- ¼ cup olive oil
- 2½ cups all-purpose flour
- 2½ tsp. baking powder
- ½ tsp. garlic powder
- ¼ tsp. salt
- ¾ cup shredded Parmesan cheese, divided
  Optional: Marinara sauce and fresh basil leaves

1. Preheat oven to 425°. Heat a 10-in. cast-iron or ovenproof skillet over medium-high heat. Add pepperoni and onion; cook and stir until pepperoni is crisp and onion is tender, 6-8 minutes. Remove and keep warm. In a large bowl, beat egg, milk, yogurt and oil until well blended. In another bowl, whisk flour, baking powder, garlic powder and salt; gradually beat into egg mixture. Stir in ½ cup cheese and the pepperoni mixture (batter will be thick).
2. Transfer to same skillet; sprinkle with remaining ¼ cup cheese. Bake until golden brown and a toothpick inserted in center comes out clean, 20-25 minutes. Cool for 10 minutes in skillet on a wire rack. Serve warm. If desired, serve with marinara sauce and top with fresh basil leaves.
1 slice: 339 cal., 18g fat (6g sat. fat), 47mg chol., 580mg sod., 33g carb. (3g sugars, 1g fiber), 12g pro.

BARBECUED
MEATBALLS

BARBECUED MEATBALLS

Grape jelly and chili sauce are the secret ingredients that make these meatballs so fantastic. If I'm serving them at a party, I prepare the meatballs and sauce in advance and reheat them right before guests arrive.
—*Irma Schnuelle, Manitowoc, WI*

Prep: 20 min. • **Cook:** 15 min.
Makes: about 3 dozen

- ½ cup dry bread crumbs
- ⅓ cup finely chopped onion
- ¼ cup 2% milk
- 1 large egg, lightly beaten
- 1 Tbsp. minced fresh parsley
- 1 tsp. salt
- 1 tsp. Worcestershire sauce
- ½ tsp. pepper
- 1 lb. lean ground beef (90% lean)
- ¼ cup canola oil
- 1 bottle (12 oz.) chili sauce
- 1 jar (10 oz.) grape jelly

1. In a bowl, combine the first 8 ingredients. Crumble beef over mixture and mix lightly but thoroughly. Shape beef into 1-in. balls. In a large skillet, brown the meatballs in oil on all sides.
2. Remove the meatballs and drain. In the same skillet, combine chili sauce and jelly; cook and stir over medium heat until jelly has melted. Return the meatballs to pan; heat through.
1 meatball: 71 cal., 3g fat (1g sat. fat), 13mg chol., 215mg sod., 9g carb. (7g sugars, 0 fiber), 3g pro.

TEST KITCHEN TIP

When mixing the uncooked ground beef with the bread crumbs, seasonings and other ingredients, don't be afraid to roll up your sleeves and use your hands. With clean hands, gently combine the ingredients, being careful not to overwork the meat. To prevent the mix from sticking as you form your meatballs, try lightly coating your hands with oil or water.

TUSCAN SAUSAGE
& BEAN DIP

TUSCAN SAUSAGE & BEAN DIP

Here's a spinoff of a Mexican dip I once tried. The original was wicked good, but I was going through an I'm-so-over-Mexican-dip phase and decided to switch it up by incorporating Mediterranean flavors. Take this version to a party—no one else will bring anything like it!
—*Mandy Rivers, Lexington, SC*

Prep: 25 min. • **Bake:** 20 min.
Makes: 16 servings

- 1 lb. bulk hot Italian sausage
- 1 medium onion, finely chopped
- 4 garlic cloves, minced
- ½ cup dry white wine or chicken broth
- ½ tsp. dried oregano
- ¼ tsp. salt
- ¼ tsp. dried thyme
- 1 pkg. (8 oz.) cream cheese, softened
- 1 pkg. (6 oz.) fresh baby spinach, coarsely chopped
- 1 can (15 oz.) cannellini beans, rinsed and drained
- 1 cup chopped seeded tomatoes
- 1 cup shredded part-skim mozzarella cheese
- ½ cup shredded Parmesan cheese
  Assorted crackers or toasted French bread baguette slices

1. Preheat oven to 375°. In a large skillet or ovenproof skillet, cook sausage, onion and garlic over medium heat until the sausage is no longer pink, breaking up sausage into crumbles; drain. Stir in wine, oregano, salt and thyme. Bring to a boil; cook until liquid is almost evaporated.
2. Add cream cheese; stir until melted. Stir in spinach, beans and tomatoes; cook and stir until spinach is wilted. Transfer mixture to a greased 8-in. square baking dish; if using an ovenproof skillet, leave in skillet. Sprinkle with cheeses.
3. Bake until bubbly, 20-25 minutes. Serve with crackers.
¼ cup: 200 cal., 14g fat (7g sat. fat), 41mg chol., 434mg sod., 7g carb. (2g sugars, 2g fiber), 10g pro.

BAKED CHEDDAR
EGGS & POTATOES, PAGE 23

CAST IRON
RISE & SHINE

Satisfying and fortifying breakfasts—both savory and sweet—
are the perfect match for cast iron. So break out your skillet,
griddle or Dutch oven, and start your morning right!

COUNTRY CORNCAKES

GREEK SALAD-INSPIRED QUICHE

I love using my cast-iron skillet to create this meatless family-sized Greek quiche. It makes a welcome weekend breakfast, or a quick dinner option on a weeknight—add a salad and pita bread, and your meal is on the table with little fuss and no extra dishes to wash!
—*Donna Ryan, Topsfield, MA*

- -

Prep: 20 min. • **Bake:** 20 min. + standing
Makes: 6 servings

- 1 Tbsp. olive oil
- 1 cup cherry tomatoes, halved
- ⅔ cup finely chopped green pepper
- ½ cup thinly sliced red onion
- ⅔ cup chopped fresh spinach
- 2 garlic cloves, minced
- 1 cup crumbled feta cheese
- ½ cup pitted Greek olives, sliced
- 6 large eggs
- 1 cup 2% milk
- 1 Tbsp. minced fresh oregano or 1 tsp. dried oregano
- ½ tsp. salt
- ⅛ to ¾ tsp. crushed red pepper flakes

1. In a 9-in. cast-iron or other ovenproof skillet, heat oil over medium-high heat. Add tomatoes, green peppers and onion; cook and stir 6-7 minutes or until vegetables are tender; drain. Add spinach and garlic; cook and stir until spinach is wilted, 1-2 minutes. Remove from heat and stir in feta and olives.
2. In a large bowl, whisk eggs, milk, oregano, salt and pepper flakes until blended. Pour over vegetables.
3. Bake until a knife inserted in the center comes out clean, 20-25 minutes. Let stand 10 minutes before serving.
1 piece: 354 cal., 22g fat (9g sat. fat), 175mg chol., 778mg sod., 25g carb. (5g sugars, 2g fiber), 12g pro.

COUNTRY CORNCAKES

Although we live in a suburban area, we are lucky to have plenty of farms nearby where we can purchase fresh homegrown corn. When it's out of season, I substitute canned or frozen corn in this favorite recipe.
—*Anne Frederick, New Hartford, NY*

- -

Prep: 15 min. • **Cook:** 20 min.
Makes: 14 corncakes

- 1½ cups yellow cornmeal
- ¼ cup all-purpose flour
- 1 Tbsp. sugar
- 1 tsp. baking soda
- ½ tsp. salt
- 1 large egg, room temperature
- 1½ cups buttermilk
- 2 Tbsp. butter, melted
- 1½ cups fresh corn or frozen corn
  Sour cream, optional
- 6 bacon strips, cooked and crumbled, optional
- 2 Tbsp. minced chives, optional

1. In a small bowl, combine the first 5 ingredients; make a well in the center. In another bowl, beat the egg, buttermilk and butter; pour into the well and stir just until blended. Gently stir in the corn; do not overmix. Cover and let stand for 5 minutes.
2. Pour batter by ¼ cupfuls onto a greased cast-iron skillet or griddle over medium-high heat. Turn after 2-3 minutes or when bubbles form on top. Cook until the second side is golden brown. Top with the sour cream, bacon and chives if desired.
2 corncakes: 220 cal., 5g fat (3g sat. fat), 41mg chol., 451mg sod., 37g carb. (6g sugars, 3g fiber), 7g pro.

GREEK SALAD-INSPIRED QUICHE

DINER CORNED BEEF HASH

I created my hash to taste like a dish from a northern Arizona restaurant we always loved. We round it out with eggs and toast made from homemade bread.
—*Denise Chelpka, Phoenix, AZ*

Prep: 10 min. • **Cook:** 25 min.
Makes: 4 servings

- 1¼ lbs. potatoes (about 3 medium), cut into ½-in. cubes
- 3 Tbsp. butter
- ¾ cup finely chopped celery
- ¾ lb. cooked corned beef, cut into ½-in. cubes (about 2½ cups)
- 4 green onions, chopped
- ¼ tsp. pepper
  Dash ground cloves
- 2 Tbsp. minced fresh cilantro

1. Place potatoes in a saucepan; add water to cover. Bring to a boil. Reduce heat; cook, uncovered, just until potatoes are tender, 6-8 minutes. Drain.
2. In a large nonstick skillet, heat butter over medium-high heat. Add the celery; cook and stir until crisp-tender, 4-6 minutes. Add the potatoes; cook until lightly browned, turning occasionally, 6-8 minutes . Stir in the corned beef; cook until heated through, 1-2 minutes. Sprinkle with the green onions, pepper and cloves; cook 1-2 minutes longer. Stir in the minced cilantro.
1 cup: 407 cal., 25g fat (11g sat. fat), 106mg chol., 1059mg sod., 27g carb. (2g sugars, 4g fiber), 19g pro.

BANANA-HAZELNUT PAIN PERDU DUET

The ultimate breakfast at our house is this French toast with warm bananas and Nutella. Pass it around with confectioners' sugar, maple syrup and fresh mint.
—*Charlene Chambers, Ormond Beach, FL*

Takes: 30 min. • **Makes:** 4 servings

- 8 slices French bread (½ in. thick)
- ¼ cup cream cheese, softened
- ¼ cup Nutella
- 1 medium banana, halved lengthwise and sliced
- 4 tsp. brown sugar
- 4 large eggs
- 1 cup 2% milk
- ¼ cup hazelnut liqueur
- 2 tsp. ground cinnamon
- 2 tsp. vanilla extract
- 2 Tbsp. butter
  Optional: Confectioners' sugar, maple syrup, fresh mint leaves, additional banana slices and additional Nutella

1. On each of 4 bread slices, spread cream cheese and Nutella to within ½ in. of edges. Top with banana slices, brown sugar and remaining bread. In a shallow bowl, whisk eggs, milk, liqueur, cinnamon and vanilla.
2. In a large cast-iron or other heavy skillet, heat butter over medium-low heat. Dip both sides of sandwiches in egg mixture, allowing each side to soak for 30 seconds. Place sandwiches in skillet; toast until golden brown, 4-5 minutes on each side. If desired, serve with toppings.
1 stuffed French toast: 469 cal., 23g fat (10g sat. fat), 221mg chol., 340mg sod., 48g carb. (29g sugars, 3g fiber), 13g pro.

DINER CORNED BEEF HASH

APPLES & CREAM PANCAKE

This recipe is delicious for breakfast or brunch. I usually make a double batch because everyone wants more! With our own orchard, we have plenty of Golden Delicious and Winesap apples—they make this a true midwestern meal.
—*Ruth Schafer, Defiance, OH*

- -

Takes: 25 min. • **Makes:** 6 servings

½ cup 2% milk
2 large eggs, room temperature
½ cup all-purpose flour
¼ tsp. salt
1 to 2 Tbsp. butter
¼ cup packed brown sugar
3 oz. cream cheese, softened
½ cup sour cream
½ tsp. vanilla extract
1½ cups thinly sliced unpeeled apples
¼ cup chopped walnuts

1. In a small bowl, combine milk, eggs, flour and salt. Beat until smooth. Heat a cast-iron or ovenproof skillet in a 450° oven until hot. Add butter to the skillet; spread over entire bottom. Pour in batter; bake for 10 minutes or until golden brown.
2. Meanwhile, combine sugar and cream cheese. Blend in sour cream and vanilla. Fill pancake with ¾ cup of the cream cheese mixture and top with apples. Spread the remaining cream cheese mixture over apples and sprinkle with nuts. Cut into wedges and serve immediately.
1 piece: 265 cal., 16g fat (8g sat. fat), 108mg chol., 204mg sod., 24g carb. (14g sugars, 1g fiber), 7g pro.

SPICY BREAKFAST PIZZA

SPICY BREAKFAST PIZZA

Eggs and hash browns have extra pizazz when they're served up on a pizza pan! My family requests this fun breakfast often, and it's a snap to make with prebaked crust, so I'm happy to oblige. I adjust the heat index of the toppings to suit the taste buds of my diners.
—*Christy Hinrichs, Parkville, MO*

- -

Takes: 30 min. • **Makes:** 6 servings

2 cups frozen shredded hash brown potatoes
¼ tsp. ground cumin
¼ tsp. chili powder
2 Tbsp. canola oil, divided
4 large eggs
2 Tbsp. 2% milk
¼ tsp. salt
2 green onions, chopped
2 Tbsp. diced sweet red pepper
1 Tbsp. finely chopped jalapeno pepper
1 garlic clove, minced
1 prebaked 12-in. thin pizza crust
½ cup salsa
¾ cup shredded cheddar cheese

1. Preheat oven to 375°. In a large nonstick skillet, cook the hash browns, cumin and chili powder in 1 Tbsp. oil over medium heat until golden. Remove and keep warm.
2. In a small bowl, beat the eggs, milk and salt; set aside. In the same skillet, saute the onions, peppers and garlic in the remaining 1 Tbsp. oil until tender. Add the egg mixture. Cook and stir over medium heat until almost set. Remove from the heat.
3. Place crust on an ungreased round 14-in. cast-iron griddle or pizza pan. Spread salsa over crust. Top with the egg mixture. Sprinkle with the hash browns and cheese. Bake until cheese is melted, 8-10 minutes.
1 slice: 320 cal., 16g fat (5g sat. fat), 138mg chol., 605mg sod., 31g carb. (2g sugars, 1g fiber), 13g pro.

CAST-IRON SCRAMBLED EGGS

I love these easy cast-iron scrambled eggs, which use fresh ingredients that I usually have on hand. They make a quick and simple breakfast! This is a great meal for cooking on a grill or over a campfire, but you can just as easily make it on your stovetop.
—*Bonnie Hawkins, Elkhorn, WI*

Takes: 25 min. • **Makes:** 6 servings

- 12 large eggs
- 2 Tbsp. water
- ¼ tsp. salt
- ¼ tsp. pepper
- 2 Tbsp. butter
- ⅔ cup finely chopped sweet onion
- 1 jalapeno pepper, seeded and chopped
- 1 log (4 oz.) fresh goat cheese, crumbled
- 3 Tbsp. minced chives

1. In a large bowl, whisk the eggs, water, salt and pepper; set aside.
2. Place a 10-in. cast-iron skillet on grill rack over medium-hot heat. Melt butter in the skillet, then add the onion and jalapeno and saute until tender. Add egg mixture; cook and stir until almost set. Stir in goat cheese and chives; cook and stir until the eggs are completely set.

⅔ cup: 217 cal., 16g fat (7g sat. fat), 446mg chol., 342mg sod., 3g carb. (2g sugars, 0 fiber), 15g pro.

**CAST-IRON
SCRAMBLED EGGS**

CAMPFIRE
READY

BAKED CHEDDAR EGGS & POTATOES

I love having breakfast for dinner, especially this combo of eggs, potatoes and cheese. It starts in a skillet on the stovetop and then I pop it into the oven to bake.
—Nadine Merheb, Tucson, AZ

- -

Takes: 30 min. • **Makes:** 4 servings

- 3 Tbsp. butter
- 1½ lbs. red potatoes, chopped
- ¼ cup minced fresh parsley
- 2 garlic cloves, minced
- ¾ tsp. kosher salt
- ⅛ tsp. pepper
- 8 large eggs
- ½ cup shredded extra-sharp cheddar cheese

1. Preheat oven to 400°. In a 10-in. cast-iron or other ovenproof skillet, heat butter over medium-high heat. Add potatoes; cook and stir until golden brown and tender. Stir in parsley, garlic, salt and pepper. With the back of a spoon, make 4 wells in the potato mixture; break 2 eggs into each well.
2. Bake until egg whites are completely set and yolks begin to thicken but are not hard, 9-11 minutes. Sprinkle with cheese; bake until cheese is melted, about 1 minute.
1 serving: 395 cal., 23g fat (12g sat. fat), 461mg chol., 651mg sod., 29g carb. (3g sugars, 3g fiber), 19g pro.

SAUSAGE JOHNNYCAKE

Here's a nice hearty breakfast with plenty of old-fashioned flavor. I serve it to my bed-and-breakfast guests, who always love the cake's savory middle and maple syrup topping. It's a fine way to start the day!
—Lorraine Guyn, Calgary, AB

- -

Prep: 20 min. • **Bake:** 30 min.
Makes: 6 servings

- 1 cup cornmeal
- 2 cups buttermilk
- 12 uncooked breakfast sausage links
- 1⅓ cups all-purpose flour
- ¼ cup sugar
- 1½ tsp. baking powder
- ½ tsp. baking soda
- ½ tsp. salt
- ⅓ cup shortening
- 1 large egg, room temperature, lightly beaten
- ½ tsp. vanilla extract
   Maple syrup

1. In a small bowl, combine cornmeal and buttermilk; let stand for 10 minutes.
2. Meanwhile, in a 9-in. cast-iron skillet over medium heat, cook sausage until no longer pink; drain on paper towels. Arrange 8 links in a spokelike pattern in the same skillet or in a greased 9-in. deep-dish pie plate. Cut remaining links in half; place between the whole sausages.
3. In a large bowl, combine the flour, sugar, baking powder, baking soda and salt. Cut in shortening until the mixture resembles coarse crumbs.
4. Stir egg and vanilla into cornmeal mixture; add to the dry ingredients and stir just until blended. Pour batter over sausages.
5. Bake at 400° for 30-35 minutes or until a toothpick inserted in the center comes out clean. Serve warm, with syrup.
1 slice: 481 cal., 23g fat (7g sat. fat), 64mg chol., 940mg sod., 53g carb. (13g sugars, 2g fiber), 15g pro.

TEST KITCHEN TIP
Johnnycakes may be frozen for up to 3 months. To freeze, wrap in foil; transfer to a freezer container. To use, remove the foil and thaw johnnycakes at room temperature. Serve warm with syrup.

GERMAN APPLE
PANCAKE

UPSIDE-DOWN BACON PANCAKE

Make a big impression when you present one family-size bacon pancake. The brown sugar adds sweetness that complements the salty bacon. Use even more bacon if you'd like!
—*Mindie Hilton, Susanville, CA*

Prep: 5 min. • **Cook:** 25 min. + cooling
Makes: 6 servings

- 6   bacon strips, coarsely chopped
- ¼   cup packed brown sugar
- 2   cups complete buttermilk pancake mix
- 1½ cups water
  Optional: Maple syrup and butter

1. In a large cast-iron or other ovenproof skillet, cook bacon over medium heat until crisp. Remove bacon to paper towels with a slotted spoon. Remove drippings, reserving 2 Tbsp.. Return bacon to pan with reserved drippings; sprinkle with brown sugar.
2. In a small bowl, combine pancake mix and water just until moistened. Pour into pan.
3. Bake at 350° until a toothpick inserted in the center comes out clean, 18-20 minutes. Cool for 10 minutes before inverting onto a serving plate. Serve warm, with maple syrup and butter if desired.

1 slice: 265 cal., 9g fat (3g sat. fat), 12mg chol., 802mg sod., 41g carb. (13g sugars, 1g fiber), 6g pro.

GERMAN APPLE PANCAKE

If you're looking for a pretty dish to make when having guests for brunch, try this one. Everyone I've served it to has enjoyed it—except for one time, that is, when my husband made it following my recipe, which I'd written down incorrectly! But as long as you don't leave out the flour as I did, it'll turn out terrific.
—*Judi Van Beek, Lynden, WA*

Prep: 15 min. • **Bake:** 20 min.
Makes: 6 servings

PANCAKE
- 3   large eggs, room temperature
- 1   cup 2% milk
- ¾   cup all-purpose flour
- ½   tsp. salt
- ⅛   tsp. ground nutmeg
- 3   Tbsp. butter

TOPPING
- 2   tart baking apples, peeled and sliced
- 3   to 4 Tbsp. butter
- 2   Tbsp. sugar
  Confectioners' sugar

1. Preheat a 10-in. cast-iron skillet in a 425° oven. Meanwhile, in a blender, combine the eggs, milk, flour, salt and nutmeg; cover and process until smooth.
2. Add butter to the hot skillet; return to oven until the butter bubbles. Pour batter into skillet. Bake, uncovered, for 20 minutes or until the pancake puffs and the edges are browned and crisp.
3. For topping, in a skillet, combine the apples, butter and sugar; cook and stir over medium heat until the apples are tender. Spoon into baked pancake. Sprinkle with confectioners' sugar. Cut and serve the pancake immediately.

1 serving: 192 cal., 12g fat (7g sat. fat), 107mg chol., 273mg sod., 18g carb. (8g sugars, 1g fiber), 5g pro.

TEST KITCHEN TIP
Many fruits can be used in place of the apples. Pears, berries, peaches or plums are all delish. If you use berries, just skip the precooking step. For extra flavor, try adding a splash of almond or vanilla extract to the batter.

SWEET POTATO & EGG SKILLET

I try to incorporate nutritious sweet potatoes in my meals as often as possible, especially with breakfast! This recipe originated with the purpose of feeding my family a healthy, hearty breakfast—and it worked!
—Jeanne Larson,
Rancho Santa Margarita, CA

Takes: 25 min. • **Makes:** 4 servings

- 2   Tbsp. butter
- 2   medium sweet potatoes, peeled and shredded (about 4 cups)
- 1   garlic clove, minced
- ½   tsp. salt, divided
- ⅛   tsp. dried thyme
- 2   cups fresh baby spinach
- 4   large eggs
- ⅛   tsp. coarsely ground pepper

1. In a large cast-iron or other heavy skillet, heat the butter over low heat. Add sweet potatoes, garlic, ¼ tsp. salt and thyme; cook, covered, until potatoes are almost tender, 4-5 minutes, stirring occasionally. Stir in spinach just until wilted, 2-3 minutes.

2. With the back of a spoon, make 4 wells in the potato mixture. Break an egg into each well. Sprinkle the eggs with pepper and remaining salt. Cook, covered, on medium-low until egg whites are completely set and yolks begin to thicken but are not hard, 5-7 minutes.

1 serving: 224 cal., 11g fat (5g sat. fat), 201mg chol., 433mg sod., 24g carb. (10g sugars, 3g fiber), 8g pro. **Diabetic exchanges:** 1½ starch, 1½ fat, 1 medium-fat meat.

TEST KITCHEN TIP

If you like your eggs sunny-side up, leave the pan uncovered while they cook.

ZUCCHINI FRITTATA

When we go on car trips, I make this frittata the night before, stuff individual portions into pita bread in the morning and microwave for a minute or two. I wrap the sandwiches in a towel so down the road we can enjoy a still-warm breakfast!
  Carol Blumenberg, *Lehigh Acres, Fl*

Takes: 20 min. • **Makes:** 2 servings

- 3   large eggs
- ¼   tsp. salt
- 1   tsp. canola oil
- ½   cup chopped onion
- 1   cup coarsely shredded zucchini
- ½   cup shredded Swiss cheese
      Coarsely ground pepper, optional

1. Preheat oven to 350°. Whisk together eggs and salt.

2. In an 8-in. ovenproof skillet coated with cooking spray, heat oil over medium heat; saute onion and zucchini until onion is crisp-tender. Pour in the egg mixture; cook until almost set, 5-6 minutes. Sprinkle with cheese.

3. Bake, uncovered, until cheese is melted, 4-5 minutes. If desired, sprinkle with pepper.

1 serving: 261 cal., 18g fat (8g sat. fat), 304mg chol., 459mg sod., 7g carb. (3g sugars, 1g fiber), 18g pro.

SWEET POTATO
& EGG SKILLET

CAMPFIRE HASH

CAMPFIRE READY

CAMPFIRE HASH

In our area we are able to camp almost all year-round. My family invented this recipe using ingredients we all love so we could enjoy them on the campfire. This hearty meal tastes so good after a full day of outdoor activities.
—*Janet Danilow, Winkleman, AZ*

- -

Prep: 15 min. • **Cook:** 40 min.
Makes: 6 servings

- 1   large onion, chopped
- 2   Tbsp. canola oil
- 2   garlic cloves, minced
- 4   large potatoes,
      peeled and cubed (about 2 lbs.)
- 1   lb. smoked kielbasa or Polish
      sausage, halved and sliced
- 1   can (4 oz.) chopped green chiles
- 1   can (15¼ oz.) whole kernel corn,
      drained

1. In a large ovenproof skillet over medium heat, cook and stir onion in oil under tender. Add garlic; cook 1 minute longer. Add the potatoes. Cook, uncovered, for 20 minutes, stirring occasionally.
2. Add kielbasa; cook and stir until meat and potatoes are tender and browned, 10-15 minutes. Stir in the chiles and corn; heat through.
1 serving: 535 cal., 26g fat (8g sat. fat), 51mg chol., 1097mg sod., 57g carb. (10g sugars, 6g fiber), 17g pro.

HOT FRUIT & SAUSAGE

I love making this easy side dish with weekend breakfasts for my family. It pairs well with the savory items I usually make at breakfast time.
—*Marian Peterson, Wisconsin Rapids, WI*

- -

Takes: 10 min. • **Makes:** 6 servings

- 1   pkg. (12 oz.) uncooked
      pork sausage links
- ¾   cup pineapple tidbits
- 2   Tbsp. brown sugar
      Pinch ground cinnamon
- 1   medium firm banana, sliced

In a large cast-iron or other heavy skillet, cook sausage according to the package directions; drain. Add pineapple, brown sugar and cinnamon; heat through. Stir in banana just before serving.
1 serving: 261 cal., 18g fat (6g sat. fat), 47mg chol., 736mg sod., 14g carb. (12g sugars, 1g fiber), 11g pro.

BRUNCH BEIGNETS

BRUNCH BEIGNETS

Enjoy breakfast the New Orleans way with these warm, crispy bites. Topped with powdered sugar, they are a delight!
—*Lois Rutherford, Elkton, FL*

- -

Prep: 20 min. + standing • **Cook:** 5 min./batch
Makes: about 2 dozen

- 2   large eggs, separated
- 1¼ cups all-purpose flour
- 1   tsp. baking powder
- ⅛   tsp. salt
- ½   cup sugar
- ¼   cup water
- 1   Tbsp. butter, melted
- 2   tsp. grated lemon zest
- 1   tsp. vanilla extract
- 1   tsp. brandy, optional
       Oil for deep-fat frying
       Confectioners' sugar

1. Place egg whites in a small bowl; let stand at room temperature for 30 minutes.
2. Meanwhile, in a large bowl, combine the flour, baking powder and salt.
3. In a second bowl, combine the egg yolks, sugar, water, butter, lemon zest, vanilla and, if desired, brandy; stir into dry ingredients just until combined.
4. Beat egg whites on medium speed until soft peaks form; fold into batter.
5. In a cast-iron or electric skillet, heat oil to 375°. Drop batter by teaspoonfuls, a few at a time, into hot oil. Fry until golden brown, about 1½ minutes on each side. Drain on paper towels. Dust with confectioners' sugar. Serve warm.
1 piece: 66 cal., 3g fat (1g sat. fat), 17mg chol., 42mg sod., 9g carb. (4g sugars, 0 fiber), 1g pro.

ORZO WITH PARMESAN
& BASIL, PAGE 35

CAST IRON
SIDES & BREADS

Rounding out menus using a heavy-duty skillet is so easy,
you'll want to do it all the time. Keep yours in mind
for these rave-winning rolls, veggies and more!

PULL-APART
HERB BREAD

PULL-APART HERB BREAD

The ingredients for this bread are so simple and the results so amazing, I'm always happy to share the secret. It's actually a variation of a doughnut recipe I made years ago using refrigerated biscuits. Tear apart this cheesy treat while it's still warm and enjoy!
—*Evelyn Kenney, Hamilton, NJ*

Takes: 30 min. • **Makes:** 8 servings

- 1 garlic clove, minced
- ¼ cup butter, melted
- 2 tubes (10.2 oz. each) refrigerated biscuits
- 1 cup shredded cheddar cheese
- ¼ tsp. dried basil
- ¼ tsp. fennel seed
- ¼ tsp. dried oregano

1. In a 10-in. cast-iron or other ovenproof skillet, saute garlic in butter for 1 minute; remove from pan and set aside. Separate the biscuits; cut biscuits in half horizontally. Place half in an even layer in the skillet, overlapping as necessary. Brush with butter mixture; sprinkle with half of the cheese and herbs. Repeat.

2. Bake at 375° 20-25 minutes or until golden brown. Cool on wire rack; serve warm.

1 piece: 220 cal., 15g fat (8g sat. fat), 30mg chol., 487mg sod., 16g carb., (2g sugars, 1g fiber), 5g pro.

TEST KITCHEN TIP
Pull-Apart Herb Bread can also be prepared in a 9-in. springform pan. Just melt the butter and combine it with the garlic beforehand, then proceed with the recipe as directed.

LEEKS IN
MUSTARD SAUCE

LEEKS IN MUSTARD SAUCE

With their delicious onion flavor, leeks can make a wonderful side dish. This one features a complementary mustard sauce for a taste that goes well with many different entrees.
—*Taste of Home Test Kitchen*

Prep: 15 min. • **Cook:** 20 min.
Makes: 8 servings

- 10 medium leeks (white portion only)
- 2 green onions with tops, chopped
- 1 garlic clove, minced
- 1 Tbsp. olive oil

MUSTARD SAUCE
- 3 large egg yolks
- ¼ cup water
- 2 Tbsp. lemon juice
- 6 Tbsp. cold butter
- 1 Tbsp. Dijon mustard
  Dash white pepper

1. Cut leeks into 1½-in. slices, then julienne. In a large cast-iron or other heavy skillet, saute leeks, green onions and garlic in oil until tender.

2. Meanwhile, in a small heavy saucepan, whisk the egg yolks, water and lemon juice. Cook and stir over low heat until mixture begins to thicken, bubbles around the edges and reaches 160°, about 20 minutes. Add the butter, 1 Tbsp. at a time, whisking after each addition until melted. Remove from the heat; stir in mustard and pepper.

3. Transfer leek mixture to a serving bowl; top with mustard sauce.

½ cup with about 4 tsp. sauce: 185 cal., 13g fat (6g sat. fat), 103mg chol., 160mg sod., 17g carb. (5g sugars, 2g fiber), 3g pro.

PATRIOTIC POTATOES WITH MUSTARD SAUCE

Show your true colors with a bowl of red, white and blue potatoes paired with a terrific homemade sauce. This dish is a star among my patriotic recipes!
—*Julie Murphy, Peachtree City, GA*

Prep: 10 min. • **Bake:** 30 min.
Makes: 8 servings

- 8   small red potatoes
- 8   small white potatoes
- 8   small blue potatoes
- 3   Tbsp. canola oil
- 1   garlic clove, minced
- ¼   tsp. salt
- ¼   tsp. dried basil
- ⅛   tsp. pepper

SAUCE

- 6   bacon strips, cooked and crumbled
- ⅔   cup sour cream
- ⅓   cup mayonnaise
- ¼   cup stone-ground mustard
- 1   Tbsp. brown sugar
- 2   tsp. minced fresh chives
- ¼   tsp. paprika

1. Preheat oven to 425°. Toss together the first 8 ingredients. Transfer to a large cast-iron skillet or shallow roasting pan. Roast 30-35 minutes or until potatoes are tender, stirring occasionally.
2. Mix the sauce ingredients. Serve sauce with the potatoes.

3 potatoes with about 2 Tbsp. sauce: 300 cal., 19g fat (4g sat. fat), 23mg chol., 402mg sod., 26g carb. (4g sugars, 3g fiber), 6g pro.

SOCCA

5i
SOCCA

Here's a traditional (and gluten-free!) flatbread from Nice, France. It's common there to see socca cooked on grills as street food, served chopped in a paper cone and sprinkled with salt, pepper or other toppings. Look for chickpea flour in your local grocery store or make your own.
—*Taste of Home Test Kitchen*

Prep: 5 min. + standing • **Cook:** 5 minutes
Makes: 6 servings

- 1   cup chickpea flour
- 1   cup water
- 2   Tbsp. extra virgin olive oil, divided
- ¾   tsp. salt
       Optional toppings: Za'atar seasoning, sea salt flakes, coarsely ground pepper and additional extra virgin olive oil

1. In a small bowl, whisk the chickpea flour, water, 1 Tbsp. oil and salt until smooth. Let stand 30 minutes.
2. Meanwhile, preheat broiler. Place a 10-in. cast-iron skillet in oven until hot, about 5 minutes. Add remaining 1 Tbsp. oil to the pan; swirl to coat. Pour batter into the hot pan and tilt to coat evenly.
3. Broil 6 in. from heat until the edges are crisp and browned and the center just begins to brown, 5-7 minutes. Cut into wedges. If desired, top with optional ingredients.

1 wedge: 113 cal., 6g fat (1g sat. fat), 0 chol., 298mg sod., 12g carb. (2g sugars, 3g fiber), 4g pro. **Diabetic exchanges:** 1 fat, ½ starch.

TEST KITCHEN TIP

To make chickpea flour, simply add dried chickpeas to a food processor. Cover and process until powdery, 2-3 minutes, then sift through a fine sieve into a bowl. Add larger pieces left in the sieve to a coffee or spice grinder; process until powdery.

FRUITY PULL-APART BREAD

Who doesn't like to start the morning with fresh-baked monkey bread? I top my skillet version with sweet-tangy berries and dollops of rich cream cheese. A sprinkle of minced basil brings it all together.
—Darla Andrews, Schertz, TX

- -

Prep: 15 min. • **Bake:** 35 min.
Makes: 8 servings

- 1 tube (16.3 oz.) large refrigerated flaky honey butter biscuits
- ½ cup packed dark brown sugar
- ½ cup sugar
- ⅓ cup butter, melted
- 1 cup fresh blueberries
- 1 cup chopped fresh strawberries
- 4 oz. cream cheese, softened
- 1 Tbsp. minced fresh basil

1. Preheat oven to 350°. Separate dough into 8 biscuits; cut biscuits into fourths.
2. In a shallow bowl, combine the sugars. Dip biscuits in melted butter, then in sugar mixture. Place biscuits in a greased 10¼-in. cast-iron skillet. Top with berries; dollop with cream cheese. Bake until biscuits are golden brown and cooked through, 35-40 minutes. Sprinkle with basil.
1 serving: 383 cal., 20g fat (9g sat. fat), 30mg chol., 641mg sod., 49g carb. (28g sugars, 2g fiber), 5g pro.

FRUITY PULL-APART BREAD

SPICY PUMPKIN FRITTERS

My husband has never been crazy about pumpkin, but when he tried these deep-fried bites, he fell in love. I serve them with chipotle mayo or ranch dressing.
—Trisha Kruse, Eagle, ID

- -

Prep: 10 min. • **Cook:** 5 min./batch
Makes: about 3 dozen

- 1½ cups all-purpose flour
- 2 tsp. baking powder
- 1¼ tsp. salt
- ¾ tsp. chili powder
- ½ tsp. onion powder
- ¼ tsp. crushed red pepper flakes
- 2 large eggs
- 1 can (15 oz.) pumpkin
- ½ cup 2% milk
- 2 Tbsp. butter, melted
  Oil for deep-fat frying
  Chipotle mayonnaise, optional

1. In a large bowl, whisk first 6 ingredients. In another bowl, whisk eggs, pumpkin, milk and melted butter until blended. Add to dry ingredients, stirring just until moistened.
2. In a deep cast-iron skillet or deep-fat fryer, heat oil to 375°. Drop the batter by tablespoonfuls, a few at a time, into the hot oil. Fry each side or until golden brown, 1½-2 minutes. Drain on paper towels. Serve warm. If desired, serve the fritters with chipotle mayonnaise.
1 fritter: 50 cal., 3g fat (1g sat. fat), 11mg chol., 105mg sod., 5g carb. (1g sugars, 0 fiber), 1g pro.

OYSTER SAUSAGE STUFFING

I always prepare this wonderful stuffing during the holidays. But it's so rich and buttery, we can't resist having it with pork roast and chops at other times of year, too.
—*Page Alexander, Baldwin City, KS*

- -

Prep: 35 min. • **Bake:** 40 min.
Makes: 9 cups (enough to stuff an 8- to 10-lb. turkey)

- 1 envelope onion soup mix
- 2 cups boiling water
- ½ cup butter, cubed
- 10 cups cubed day-old bread, toasted
- 1 can (8 oz.) whole oysters, drained
- ½ lb. bulk pork sausage, cooked and drained
- ½ cup minced fresh parsley
- ¾ tsp. poultry seasoning

1. Place onion soup mix in a bowl; add boiling water and let stand for 5 minutes. In a Dutch oven, melt butter. Stir in the bread cubes and soup mixture. Cover and cook over low heat for 5 minutes, stirring occasionally. Gently stir in the oysters, sausage, parsley and poultry seasoning.

2. Transfer to a large greased cast-iron skillet or 2½-qt. baking dish. Cover and bake at 375° until heated through, 40-50 minutes.

¾ cup: 228 cal., 13g fat (6g sat. fat), 38mg chol., 590mg sod., 22g carb. (2g sugars, 1g fiber), 6g pro.

OYSTER SAUSAGE STUFFING

ORZO WITH PARMESAN & BASIL

Dried basil, grated Parmesan and just a few other ingredients add lots of flavor to orzo pasta. The deliciously creamy side dish is ready to serve in only 20 minutes.
—*Anna Chaney, Antigo, WI*

- -

Takes: 20 min. • **Makes:** 4 servings

- 1 cup uncooked orzo pasta or pearl couscous
- 2 Tbsp. butter
- 1 can (14½ oz.) chicken broth
- ½ cup grated Parmesan cheese
- 2 tsp. dried basil
- ⅛ tsp. pepper
  Thinly sliced fresh basil, optional

1. In a large cast-iron or other heavy skillet, saute orzo in butter until lightly browned, 3-5 minutes.
2. Stir in broth. Bring to a boil. Reduce heat; cover and simmer until liquid is absorbed and orzo is tender, 10-15 minutes. Stir in cheese, dried basil and pepper. If desired, top with fresh basil.

½ cup: 285 cal., 10g fat (5g sat. fat), 26mg chol., 641mg sod., 38g carb. (2g sugars, 1g fiber), 11g pro.

Corn & Pepper Orzo: Omit the Parmesan cheese, basil and pepper. Prepare the orzo as directed. In a large skillet coated with cooking spray, saute 1 chopped large red sweet pepper and 1 chopped medium onion in 1 Tbsp. olive oil. Stir in 2 cups thawed frozen corn, 2 tsp. Italian seasoning and ⅛ tsp. each salt and pepper. Drain orzo; toss with vegetable mixture. Yield: 6 servings.

TOMATO-BASIL PULL-APART ROLLS

My young nephew helped me create these soft, colorful skillet treats. He called them "wheelies" because their spiral shape reminded him of his toy trucks!
—*Dianna Wara, Washington, IL*

- -

Prep: 30 min. + rising • **Bake:** 20 min.
Makes: 1 dozen

- 1 pkg. (¼ oz.) active dry yeast
- 2 Tbsp. sugar
- ¾ cup warm 2% milk (110° to 115°)
- 1 large egg, room temperature
- ¼ cup tomato paste
- 3 Tbsp. olive oil
- 1 tsp. salt
- 2¾ to 3¼ cups bread flour

FILLING
- 1 cup shredded Italian cheese blend
- 2 tsp. dried basil
- ½ tsp. garlic powder

1. Dissolve yeast and sugar in warm milk. In a large bowl, beat egg, tomato paste, oil, salt, yeast mixture and 1 cup bread flour on medium speed until smooth. Stir in enough remaining flour to form a soft dough (dough will be sticky)
2. Turn dough onto a floured surface; knead until smooth and elastic, 6-8 minutes. Place in a greased bowl, turning to grease the top. Cover; let rise in a warm place until doubled, about 45 minutes.
3. In a bowl, toss filling ingredients. Punch down dough, turn onto a lightly floured surface. Roll into a 16x12-in. rectangle. Sprinkle with filling to within ½ in. of edges. Roll up jelly-roll style, starting with a long side; pinch seam to seal. Cut into 12 slices.
4. Place, cut side down, in a parchment-lined 10-in. cast-iron skillet. Cover with a kitchen towel; let rise in a warm place until almost doubled, about 45 minutes. Preheat oven to 350°.
5. Bake until golden brown, 20-25 minutes. Remove rolls to a wire rack.

Freeze option: Securely wrap cooled rolls in foil; place in an airtight container. To use, partially thaw overnight in the refrigerator. Reheat rolls, wrapped in foil, in a preheated 300° oven until warm, about 25 minutes.

1 roll: 204 cal., 7g fat (2g sat. fat), 24mg chol., 284mg sod., 27g carb. (3g sugars, 1g fiber), 7g pro.

PARMESAN-BACON BUBBLE BREAD

When I was looking for something to make with leftover bread dough, I started with a recipe I often use for bubble bread and replaced the sweet ingredients with savory. We loved the result!
—*Lori McLain, Denton, TX*

Prep: 20 min. + rising • **Bake:** 20 min.
Makes: 16 servings

- 1 loaf frozen bread dough, thawed (16 oz.)
- ¼ cup butter, melted
- ¾ cup shredded Parmesan cheese
- 6 bacon strips, cooked and finely crumbled, divided
- ⅓ cup finely chopped green onions, divided
- 2 Tbsp. grated Parmesan cheese
- 2 Tbsp. salt-free herb seasoning blend
- 1½ tsp. sugar
  Optional: Alfredo sauce or marinara sauce

1. Turn dough onto a lightly floured surface; divide and shape into 16 rolls. Place butter in a shallow bowl. In a large bowl, combine shredded Parmesan, half the bacon, half the green onions, grated Parmesan, seasoning blend and sugar. Dip dough pieces in butter, then toss with cheese mixture to coat. Stack pieces in a greased 9-in. cast-iron skillet.
2. Cover with a kitchen towel; let rise in a warm place until almost doubled, about 45 minutes. Preheat oven to 350°. Bake until golden brown, 20-25 minutes. Top with the remaining bacon and green onions. Serve warm and, if desired, with Alfredo sauce or marinara sauce.

1 piece: 140 cal., 6g fat (3g sat. fat), 14mg chol., 311mg sod., 14g carb. (2g sugars, 1g fiber), 6g pro.

TEST KITCHEN TIP
Using your cast-iron skillet to prepare something else? Parmesan-Bacon Bubble Bread can be baked in a greased 9x5-in. loaf pan as well.

KALE & FENNEL SKILLET

KALE & FENNEL SKILLET

I'm always combining different veggies, herbs and spices in my cooking to change things up. This skillet is a good example! The big chunks of sausage make it an especially hearty and satisfying side dish.
—*Patricia Levenson, Santa Ana, CA*

Prep: 10 min. • **Cook:** 25 min.
Makes: 6 servings

- 2 Tbsp. extra virgin olive oil
- 1 small onion, thinly sliced
- 1 small fennel bulb, thinly sliced
- ½ lb. fully cooked apple chicken sausage links or cooked Italian sausage links, halved lengthwise and sliced into half-moons
- 2 garlic cloves, minced
- 3 Tbsp. dry sherry or dry white wine
- 1 Tbsp. herbes de Provence
- ⅛ tsp. salt
- ⅛ tsp. pepper
- 1 bunch kale, trimmed and torn into bite-sized pieces

1. In a large cast-iron or other heavy skillet, heat olive oil over medium-high heat. Add onion and fennel; cook and stir until onion begins to brown, 6-8 minutes. Add sausage, garlic, sherry and seasonings; cook until sausage starts to caramelize, 4-6 minutes.
2. Add the kale; cook, covered, stirring occasionally, until the kale is tender, 15-17 minutes.
¾ cup: 167 cal., 8g fat (2g sat. fat), 27mg chol., 398mg sod., 16g carb. (6g sugars, 3g fiber), 9g pro. **Diabetic exchanges:** 2 vegetable, 1 lean meat, 1 fat.

PARMESAN-BACON
BUBBLE BREAD

JALAPENO BUTTERMILK CORNBREAD

If you're from the South, a good cornbread recipe is a must. Here's a lighter take on my mother's traditional version. I love that I can cut calories and still indulge.
—*Debi Mitchell, Flower Mound, TX*

- -

Prep: 15 min. • **Bake:** 20 min.
Makes: 8 servings

1	cup self-rising flour
1	cup yellow cornmeal
1	cup buttermilk
¼	cup egg substitute
3	Tbsp. canola oil, divided
2	Tbsp. honey
1	Tbsp. reduced-fat mayonnaise
¼	cup fresh or frozen corn, thawed
3	Tbsp. shredded reduced-fat cheddar cheese
3	Tbsp. finely chopped sweet red pepper
½	to 1 jalapeno pepper, seeded and finely chopped

1. Preheat oven to 425°. In a large bowl, whisk flour and cornmeal. In another bowl, whisk buttermilk, egg substitute, 2 Tbsp. oil, honey and mayonnaise. Pour remaining oil into an 8-in. cast-iron or other ovenproof skillet; place skillet in oven 4 minutes.
2. Meanwhile, add the buttermilk mixture to the flour mixture; stir just until moistened. Fold in corn, cheese and peppers.
3. Carefully tilt and rotate the skillet to coat the bottom with oil; add batter. Bake until a toothpick inserted in the center comes out clean, 20-25 minutes. Serve warm.
1 wedge: 180 cal., 4g fat (1g sat. fat), 4mg chol., 261mg sod., 32g carb. (6g sugars, 2g fiber), 6g pro. **Diabetic exchanges:** 2 starch, 1 fat.
Note: As a substitute for 1 cup of self-rising flour, place 1½ tsp. baking powder and ½ tsp. salt in a measuring cup. Add all-purpose flour to measure 1 cup. Wear disposable gloves when cutting hot peppers; the oils can burn skin. Avoid touching your face.

RAINBOW HASH

To encourage people to eat outside their veggie comfort zone, I use lots of color. This hash for two combines sweet potato, carrot, purple potato and kale.
—*Courtney Stultz, Weir, KS*

- -

Takes: 30 min. • **Makes:** 2 servings

2	Tbsp. olive or coconut oil
1	medium sweet potato, peeled and cubed
1	medium purple potato, peeled and cubed
1	large carrot, peeled and cubed
½	tsp. dried oregano
½	tsp. dried basil
½	tsp. sea salt
½	tsp. pepper
2	cups coarsely chopped fresh kale or spinach
1	small garlic clove, minced

In a large skillet, heat the oil over medium heat. Cook and stir potatoes, carrot and seasonings until the vegetables are tender, 10-12 minutes. Add kale and garlic; continue cooking until vegetables are lightly browned and kale is tender, 2-4 minutes.
1 cup: 304 cal., 14g fat (2g sat. fat), 0 chol., 523mg sod., 43g carb. (12g sugars, 5g fiber), 4g pro.

JALAPENO BUTTERMILK CORNBREAD

ORANGE-GLAZED CARROTS, ONIONS & RADISHES

We never have leftovers when I make this sweet, spicy, crunchy side. If you prepare it ahead of time, reheat it and sprinkle on the walnuts just before serving.
—*Thomas Faglon, Somerset, NJ*

Prep: 15 min. • **Cook:** 20 min.
Makes: 8 servings

- 1   lb. fresh pearl onions
- ¼   cup butter, cubed
- 2   lbs. medium carrots, thinly sliced
- 12 radishes, thinly sliced
- ½   cup dark brown sugar
- 4   tsp. grated orange zest
- ½   cup orange juice
- 1   cup chopped walnuts, toasted

1. In a large saucepan, bring 4 cups water to a boil. Add pearl onions; boil 3 minutes. Drain and rinse with cold water. Peel.
2. In a large skillet, heat the butter over medium heat. Add carrots, pearl onions, radishes, brown sugar, orange zest and juice; cook, covered, until the vegetables are tender, stirring occasionally, 10-15 minutes. Cook, uncovered, until slightly thickened, 5-7 minutes longer. Sprinkle with walnuts.
¾ cup: 277 cal., 16g fat (5g sat. fat), 15mg chol., 141mg sod., 34g carb. (23g sugars, 5g fiber), 4g pro.

EASY CAST-IRON
PEACH BISCUIT ROLLS

EASY CAST-IRON PEACH BISCUIT ROLLS

I used to go to the local coffee shop for fresh peach cinnamon rolls, but as a busy mom, I no longer have time. So I came up with my own no-yeast treats. They're quick and easy for me to bake at home!
—*Heather Karow, Burnett, WI*

Prep: 25 min. • **Bake:** 25 min. + cooling
Makes: 1 dozen

- 1   cup packed brown sugar
- ¼   cup butter, softened
- 3   tsp. ground cinnamon

DOUGH
- 2   cups all-purpose flour
- 2   Tbsp. sugar
- 1   Tbsp. baking powder
- 1   tsp. salt
- 3   Tbsp. butter
- ¾   cup 2% milk
- 1   can (15 oz.) sliced peaches in juice, undrained
- 1   cup confectioners' sugar

1. Preheat oven to 350°. In a small bowl, mix the brown sugar, butter and cinnamon until crumbly. Reserve half for the topping. Sprinkle the remaining crumb mixture onto the bottom of a 10-in. cast-iron or other ovenproof skillet.
2. For dough, in a large bowl, mix flour, sugar, baking powder and salt. Cut in butter until crumbly. Add milk; stir to form a soft dough (dough will be sticky). Roll into an 18x12-in. rectangle. Sprinkle the reserved topping to within ½ in. of the edges.
3. Drain peaches, reserving 2 Tbsp. juice for glaze. Chop peaches; place over the topping. Roll up jelly-roll style, starting with a long side; pinch seam to seal. Cut into 12 slices. Place in prepared skillet, cut side down.
4. Bake until lightly browned, 25-30 minutes. Cool on a wire rack 10 minutes. For glaze, combine confectioners' sugar and 1-2 Tbsp. reserved peach juice to reach the desired consistency. Drizzle over warm rolls.
1 roll: 279 cal., 7g fat (4g sat. fat), 19mg chol., 746mg sod., 52g carb. (35g sugars, 1g fiber), 3g pro.

CANNELLINI BAKED BEANS

My sister came up with this unexpected side after a Christmas holiday. We were all still together, but nobody wanted to go to the grocery store. So we made do with what we found in the kitchen. This creation was great! If you'd like, try a combination of beans, such as half black beans and half white.
—*Debra Keil, Owasso, OK*

- -

Prep: 25 min. • **Bake:** 20 min.
Makes: 6 servings

- 3   bacon strips, chopped
- 1   medium onion, chopped
- 3   garlic cloves, minced
- 2   cans (15 oz. each) cannellini beans, rinsed and drained
- ⅔   cup beer or chicken broth
- ¼   cup packed brown sugar
- 2   Tbsp. balsamic vinegar
- 2   Tbsp. tomato paste
- 1   Tbsp. Dijon mustard
- 1   tsp. Worcestershire sauce
- ¼   tsp. salt
- ¼   tsp. minced fresh thyme or ⅛ tsp. dried thyme
- ⅛   tsp. pepper

Preheat oven to 400°. In a 10-in. cast-iron or other ovenproof skillet, cook bacon over medium heat until crisp, stirring occasionally. Remove with a slotted spoon; drain on paper towels. Cook and stir the onion in the bacon drippings until tender, 5-6 minutes. Add the garlic; cook 1 minute longer. Stir in remaining ingredients and the reserved bacon; bring to a boil. Place skillet in oven. Bake until bubbly and sauce is slightly thickened, 20-25 minutes.

⅔ cup: 228 cal., 6g fat (2g sat. fat), 9mg chol., 444mg sod., 34g carb. (12g sugars, 6g fiber), 8g pro.

CANNELLINI BAKED BEANS

GRANNY'S APPLE SCALLOPED POTATOES

I enjoy scalloped potatoes and apples so much, I created my own dish. I think it goes perfectly with breaded baked pork chops—which you could cook at the same time in another cast-iron pan! We're retired and my recipe makes enough for the two of us, but it's easy to double as well.
—*Shirley Rickis, The Villages, FL*

Prep: 25 min. • **Bake:** 55 min. + standing
Makes: 4 servings

- 1 medium Granny Smith apple, peeled and thinly sliced
- 1 tsp. sugar
- 1 tsp. lemon juice
- 2 Tbsp. butter
- ½ cup sliced sweet onion
- 4 medium red potatoes, thinly sliced (about 1 lb.)
- ¾ cup plus 2 Tbsp. shredded Parmesan cheese, divided
- ½ cup heavy whipping cream
- ½ tsp. minced fresh thyme or ¼ tsp. dried thyme
- ¼ tsp. salt
- ¼ tsp. pepper
- 4 bacon strips, cooked and crumbled
  Chopped fresh parsley, optional

Preheat oven to 350°. In a small bowl, combine apple slices, sugar and lemon juice; toss to coat. Set aside. In an 8- or 9-in. cast-iron or other ovenproof skillet, heat butter over medium heat. Add onion; cook and stir until crisp-tender, about 3 minutes. Remove from the heat. Alternately arrange potato and apple slices in a single layer in same skillet. Combine ¾ cup Parmesan cheese, cream, thyme, salt and pepper; pour over top. Bake, uncovered, 50 minutes. Top with bacon and remaining 2 Tbsp. Parmesan cheese. Bake until potatoes are tender and top is lightly browned, 5-10 minutes longer. Let stand 10 minutes before serving. If desired, sprinkle with parsley.
1 serving: 376 cal., 25g fat (15g sat. fat), 70mg chol., 651mg sod., 27g carb. (7g sugars, 3g fiber), 13g pro.

LEMON RICOTTA FRITTERS

It's impossible to resist these golden brown treats. Soft and cakelike inside, they have a lovely flavor combination of tangy lemon and rich ricotta cheese.
—*Tina Mirilovich, Johnstown, PA*

Takes: 30 min. • **Makes:** about 2 dozen

- 1 cup all-purpose flour
- 2 tsp. baking powder
- 1½ tsp. grated lemon zest
  Pinch salt
- 3 large eggs
- 1 cup whole-milk ricotta cheese
- 3 Tbsp. sugar
- ½ tsp. lemon extract
  Oil for deep-fat frying
  Confectioners' sugar
  Honey or strawberry jam

1. In a large bowl, whisk flour, baking powder, lemon zest and salt. In another bowl, whisk eggs, cheese, sugar and extract. Add to dry ingredients, stirring just until moistened.
2. In a deep cast-iron skillet or deep-fat fryer, heat the oil to 375°. Drop the batter by tablespoonfuls, several at a time, into hot oil. Fry 2-3 minutes or until golden brown. Drain on paper towels. Dust with confectioners' sugar. Serve warm with honey or jam.
1 fritter: 60 cal., 3g fat (1g sat. fat), 24mg chol., 58mg sod., 5g carb. (2g sugars, 0 fiber), 2g pro.

"These are wonderful with coffee. I add just a pinch of nutmeg and top them with a little honey and powdered sugar."
NACY, TASTEOFHOME.COM

SKILLET BOW TIE
LASAGNA, PAGE 54

CAST IRON
BEEF & GROUND BEEF

If you're looking for dinnertime ease and stick-to-your-ribs satisfaction, you've come to the right place. These recipes turn out the hearty entrees today's home cooks rely on most.

SPICE-CRUSTED STEAKS
WITH CHERRY SAUCE

MEATBALL CHILI
WITH DUMPLINGS

My family enjoys this delicious recipe—it's like a spicy meatball stew with dumplings!
—*Sarah Yoder, Middlebury, IN*

Prep: 20 min. • **Cook:** 50 min.
Makes: 6 servings

- 1 large egg, beaten
- ¾ cup finely chopped onion, divided
- ¼ cup dry bread crumbs or rolled oats
- 5 tsp. beef bouillon granules, divided
- 3 tsp. chili powder, divided
- 1 lb. ground beef
- 3 Tbsp. all-purpose flour
- 1 Tbsp. canola oil
- 1 can (28 oz.) diced tomatoes, undrained
- 1 garlic clove, minced
- ½ tsp. ground cumin
- 1 can (16 oz.) kidney beans, rinsed and drained

CORNMEAL DUMPLINGS
- 1½ cups biscuit/baking mix
- ½ cup yellow cornmeal
- ⅔ cup 2% milk
  Minced chives, optional

1. In a large bowl, combine egg, ¼ cup onion, bread crumbs, 3 tsp. bouillon and 1 tsp. chili powder; crumble beef over mixture and mix lightly but thoroughly. Shape into twelve 1½-in. meatballs. Roll in flour.
2. Heat oil in a 12-in. cast-iron or other ovenproof skillet; brown meatballs. Drain on paper towels. Wipe skillet clean with paper towels. Add tomatoes, garlic, cumin and the remaining onion, bouillon and chili powder to skillet; stir to combine. Add meatballs. Cover and cook over low heat for about 20 minutes. Stir in beans.
3. Combine dumpling ingredients. Drop by spoonfuls onto the chili; cook on low, uncovered, for 10 minutes. Cover and cook until a toothpick inserted in dumpling comes out clean, 10-12 minutes longer. If desired, sprinkle with minced chives.
1 serving: 475 cal., 16g fat (6g sat. fat), 76mg chol., 1523mg sod., 56g carb. (8g sugars, 7g fiber), 26g pro.

SPICE-CRUSTED STEAKS
WITH CHERRY SAUCE

If you're hosting a few meat lovers, these impressive cast-iron skillet steaks are sure to please. They're perfect for a special-occasion dinner but with the convenience of a weeknight staple.
—*Taste of Home Test Kitchen*

Prep: 20 min. + chilling • **Cook:** 45 min.
Makes: 4 servings

- ½ cup dried cherries
- ¼ cup port wine, warmed
- 3½ tsp. coarsely ground pepper
- 1 tsp. brown sugar
- ¾ tsp. garlic powder
- ¾ tsp. paprika
- ¾ tsp. ground coffee
- ½ tsp. kosher salt
- ¼ tsp. ground cinnamon
- ¼ tsp. ground cumin
- ⅛ tsp. ground mustard
- 4 beef tenderloin steaks (1¼ in. thick and 6 oz. each)
- 1 Tbsp. canola oil
- 1 large shallot, finely chopped
- 1 Tbsp. butter
- 1 cup reduced-sodium beef broth
- 1 tsp. minced fresh thyme
- ½ cup heavy whipping cream
  Crumbled blue cheese, optional

1. In a small bowl, combine cherries and wine; set aside. In a shallow dish, combine the pepper, brown sugar, garlic powder, paprika, coffee, salt, cinnamon, cumin and mustard. Add 1 steak at a time and turn to coat. Cover and refrigerate for 30 minutes.
2. Place oil in a 10-in. cast-iron or other ovenproof skillet; tilt to coat bottom. Heat oil over medium-high heat; sear the steaks, 2 minutes on each side. Bake, uncovered, at 350° until meat reaches desired doneness (for medium-rare, a thermometer should read 135°; medium, 140°; medium-well, 145°), about 15 minutes. Remove steaks and keep warm.
3. Wipe skillet clean; saute shallot in butter until crisp-tender. Add broth and thyme. Bring to a boil; cook until liquid is reduced by half, about 8 minutes. Stir in cream; bring to a boil. Cook mixture until thickened, stirring occasionally, about 8 minutes.
4. Stir in the reserved cherry mixture. Serve sauce over steaks. If desired, sprinkle with blue cheese.
1 steak with 3 Tbsp. sauce: 506 cal., 28g fat (13g sat. fat), 124mg chol., 381mg sod., 20g carb. (13g sugars, 1g fiber), 39g pro.

MEATBALL CHILI
WITH DUMPLINGS

CURRIED BEEF PITA POCKETS

If there's anyone in your family who thinks they won't like the taste of curry, serve these, and they'll be a curry lover forever!
—*Mary Ann Kosmas, Minneapolis, MN*

Prep: 5 min. • Cook: 30 min.
Makes: 4 servings

- 1   lb. ground beef
- 1   medium onion, chopped
- 1   garlic clove, halved
- 1   Tbsp. curry powder
- ½   cup water
- ½   tsp. salt
- ½   tsp. sugar
- ¼   tsp. pepper
- 1   medium tomato, seeded and diced
- 1   medium zucchini, diced
- 8   pita pocket halves
     Refrigerated tzatziki sauce, optional

1. In a large cast-iron or other heavy skillet, brown ground beef with the onion, garlic and curry; drain and discard garlic. Stir in the water, salt, sugar and pepper. Cover and simmer 15 minutes.
2. Add the tomato and zucchini; cook just until heated through. Spoon meat mixture into pita breads. If desired, serve with the tzatziki sauce.
2 filled pita halves: 393 cal., 14g fat (5g sat. fat), 70mg chol., 665mg sod., 38g carb. (4g sugars, 3g fiber), 27g pro.

TEST KITCHEN TIP
A simple switch to 90% lean ground beef would save 4 grams of fat per serving; use 95% lean to save 8 grams per serving.

CHILI SKILLET

Like most farmers, my husband loves a good hearty chili. With all of its vegetables, cheese and meat, this dish makes a super supper. Best of all, it comes together in one skillet on top of the stove. I serve it frequently in fall and winter.
—*Katherine Brown, Fredericktown, OH*

Prep: 15 min. • Cook: 40 min.
Makes: 4 servings

- 1   lb. ground beef
- 1   cup chopped onion
- ½   cup chopped green pepper
- 1   garlic clove, minced
- 1   can (16 oz.) kidney beans, rinsed and drained
- 1   cup tomato juice
- ½   cup water
- 4   tsp. chili powder
- 1   tsp. dried oregano
- 1   tsp. salt
- ½   cup uncooked long grain rice
- 1   cup canned or frozen corn
- ½   cup sliced ripe olives
- 1   cup shredded cheddar or Monterey Jack cheese
     Thinly sliced green onions, optional

1. In a large skillet over medium heat, cook ground beef, onion, pepper and garlic until the meat is no longer pink; drain. Add the next 7 ingredients; simmer, covered, until rice is tender, about 25 minutes.
2. Stir in corn and olives; cover and cook 5 minutes more. Sprinkle with cheese; cook, covered, until the cheese is melted, about 5 minutes. If desired, top with green onions.
1 serving: 599 cal., 26g fat (11g sat. fat), 98mg chol., 1557mg sod., 54g carb. (9g sugars, 10g fiber), 38g pro.

CHILI SKILLET

pepperoni, ham, olives, mozzarella and shredded Parmesan.

5. Bake until crust is golden brown and cheese is melted, 30-35 minutes. Serve with additional pizza sauce.

1 slice: 712 cal., 42g fat (19g sat. fat), 184mg chol., 1865mg sod., 48g carb. (3g sugars, 3g fiber), 36g pro.

SPANISH RICE WITH GROUND BEEF

I don't know the origin of this recipe, but it's one that has been in my family for a long time. I can remember eating it often as a little girl.
—*Beverly Austin, Fulton, MO*

Prep: 5 min. • **Cook:** 30 min.
Makes: 6 servings

- 1 lb. ground beef
- 1 cup chopped onion
- ½ cup chopped green pepper
- 1 garlic clove, minced
- 1 Tbsp. chili powder
- 1 bottle (32 oz.) tomato or vegetable juice
- 1 cup uncooked long grain rice
- ½ tsp. salt

In a skillet, brown ground beef; drain. Stir in the onion, green pepper, garlic and chili powder. Cook and stir until the vegetables are tender. Stir in remaining ingredients; bring to a boil. Reduce heat; cover and simmer for 20-30 minutes or until the rice is tender and most of the liquid is absorbed.

1 cup: 304 cal., 10g fat (4g sat. fat), 47mg chol., 662mg sod., 36g carb. (5g sugars, 2g fiber), 18g pro.

CAST-IRON FAVORITE PIZZA

Cast-iron skillets are the perfect vessel for a crisp, deep-dish pizza without buying any extra cookware. Our team developed this meaty pizza, which is perfect for any occasion at any time of year.
—Taste of Home *Test Kitchen*

Prep: 30 min. + rising • **Bake:** 30 min.
Makes: 8 slices

- 1 pkg. (¼ oz.) active dry yeast
- ½ cup warm water (110° to 115°)
- ½ cup butter, melted and cooled
- 3 large eggs, room temperature
- ¼ cup grated Parmesan cheese
- 1 tsp. salt
- 3 to 3½ cups bread flour
- 2 Tbsp. yellow cornmeal
- ½ lb. ground beef
- ½ lb. bulk Italian sausage
- 1 small onion, chopped
- 1 can (8 oz.) pizza sauce
- 1 jar (4½ oz.) sliced mushrooms, drained
- 1 pkg. (3 oz.) sliced pepperoni
- ½ lb. deli ham, cubed
- ½ cup chopped pitted green olives
- 1 can (4¼ oz.) chopped ripe olives, drained
- 1½ cups shredded part-skim mozzarella cheese
- ½ cup shredded Parmesan cheese

1. In a small bowl, dissolve yeast in warm water. In a large bowl, combine butter, eggs, grated Parmesan, salt, yeast mixture and 2 cups flour; beat on medium speed until smooth. Stir in enough remaining flour to form a soft dough.

2. Turn dough onto a floured surface; knead until smooth and elastic, 6-8 minutes. Place in a greased bowl, turning once to grease the top. Cover and let rise in a warm place until doubled, about 1 hour.

3. Punch dough down; let rest for 5 minutes. Grease a 12-in. deep-dish cast-iron skillet or other ovenproof skillet; sprinkle with cornmeal. Press dough into pan; build up edges slightly.

4. Preheat oven to 400°. In a large skillet, cook beef, sausage and onion over medium heat until meat is no longer pink and onion is tender, breaking up meat into crumbles, 8-10 minutes; drain. Spread the pizza sauce over dough to within 1 in. of edges; sprinkle with meat mixture. Top with mushrooms,

ORANGE BEEF LETTUCE WRAPS

This is a lighter version of a restaurant favorite. I also recommend trying these wraps with ground chicken or turkey.
—Robin Haas, Cranston, RI

- -

Prep: 20 min. • **Cook:** 15 min.
Makes: 8 servings

SAUCE
- ¼ cup rice vinegar
- 3 Tbsp. water
- 3 Tbsp. orange marmalade
- 1 Tbsp. sugar
- 1 Tbsp. reduced-sodium soy sauce
- 2 garlic cloves, minced
- 1 tsp. Sriracha chili sauce

WRAPS
- 1½ lbs. lean ground beef (90% lean)
- 2 garlic cloves, minced
- 2 tsp. minced fresh gingerroot
- ¼ cup reduced-sodium soy sauce
- 2 Tbsp. orange juice
- 1 Tbsp. sugar
- 1 Tbsp. orange marmalade
- ¼ tsp. crushed red pepper flakes
- 2 tsp. cornstarch
- ¼ cup cold water
- 8 Bibb or Boston lettuce leaves
- 2 cups cooked brown rice
- 1 cup shredded carrots
- 3 green onions, thinly sliced

1. In a small bowl, combine the sauce ingredients.
2. In a large skillet, cook the beef, garlic and ginger over medium heat 8-10 minutes or until the meat is no longer pink, breaking into crumbles; drain. Stir in the soy sauce, orange juice, sugar, marmalade and pepper flakes. In a small bowl, mix cornstarch and water; stir into pan. Cook and stir 1-2 minutes or until sauce is thickened.
3. Serve in lettuce leaves with rice. Top with carrots and green onions; drizzle with sauce.
1 wrap: 250 cal., 8g fat (3g sat. fat), 53mg chol., 462mg sod., 26g carb. (11g sugars, 2g fiber), 19g pro. **Diabetic exchanges:** 2 starch, 2 lean meat.

CHINESE SCALLION PANCAKE BEEF ROLLS

This is a favorite in our household, and it's perfect for using up leftover roast beef. The green-onion dough is easy to make and cooks quickly. Then, just reheat the sliced beef in a frying pan with a sweet and savory sauce, and serve!
—Carla Mendres, Winnipeg, MB

- -

Prep: 45 min. + standing • **Cook:** 40 min.
Makes: 8 servings

- 2½ cups all-purpose flour
- 1 tsp. salt
- 1 cup boiling water
- 1 bunch green onions, finely chopped
- ½ cup canola oil
- 1 Tbsp. sesame oil
- 1 small onion, thinly sliced
- 2 garlic cloves, minced
- 1 tsp. minced fresh gingerroot
- 1 pkg. (15 oz.) refrigerated beef roast au jus, drained and chopped or 2 cups chopped cooked roast beef
- 3 Tbsp. soy sauce
- 2 Tbsp. hoisin sauce
- 1 Tbsp. honey

1. Place flour and salt in a large bowl; stir in boiling water until dough forms a ball. Turn onto a floured surface; knead until smooth and elastic, 4-6 minutes. Place in a large bowl; cover and let rest for 30 minutes.
2. Divide dough into 8 portions; roll each portion into an 8-in. circle. Sprinkle each with 1 Tbsp. green onion. Roll up jelly-roll style; holding 1 end of the rope, wrap dough around, forming a coil, pinching to seal. Flatten the coils slightly. Roll each coil to ⅛-in. thickness.
3. In a large cast-iron or other heavy skillet, heat 1 Tbsp. canola oil. Cook pancakes, 1 at a time, over medium-high heat until golden brown, 2-3 minutes on each side, adding more oil as needed; keep warm.
4. In the same skillet, heat sesame oil over medium-high heat. Add onion, garlic and ginger; cook and stir 5-6 minutes or until tender. Add the remaining ingredients; cook until heated through, 3-4 minutes longer. Spoon about ¼ cup beef mixture down center of each pancake. If desired, sprinkle with some sliced green onions. Roll up tightly and serve.
1 roll: 390 cal., 20g fat (3g sat. fat), 32mg chol., 898mg sod., 37g carb. (5g sugars, 2g fiber), 16g pro.

SKILLET STEAK SUPPER

SKILLET STEAK SUPPER

With all of the ingredients cooked in one skillet, this steak dish couldn't be quicker to prepare—or clean up! But the wine and mushroom sauce makes it seem special.
—*Sandra Fisher, Missoula, MT*

- -

Takes: 20 min. • **Makes:** 2 servings

1	beef top sirloin steak (¾ lb.)
½	tsp. salt, divided
½	tsp. pepper, divided
1	Tbsp. olive oil
1	to 2 Tbsp. butter
½	lb. sliced fresh mushrooms
2	Tbsp. white wine or chicken broth
3	Tbsp. chopped green onions
1	Tbsp. Worcestershire sauce
1	tsp. Dijon mustard

1. Sprinkle steak with ¼ tsp. each salt and pepper. In a skillet, heat oil over medium-high heat; cook steak to desired doneness (for medium-rare, a thermometer should read 135°; medium, 140°), 4-6 minutes per side. Remove from pan; keep warm.

2. In same skillet, heat butter over medium-high heat; saute mushrooms until tender. Stir in wine; bring to a boil, stirring to loosen the browned bits from pan. Stir in green onions, Worcestershire sauce, mustard and the remaining salt and pepper. Cut steak in half; serve with mushroom mixture.

1 serving: 368 cal., 20g fat (7g sat. fat), 85mg chol., 915mg sod., 6g carb. (3g sugars, 2g fiber), 40g pro.

READY IN 20 MINS.

PINWHEEL
STEAK POTPIE

PINWHEEL STEAK POTPIE

On cool nights, nothing hits the spot like a steaming homemade potpie—especially one you can get on the table fast. The pinwheel crust on top has become my signature.
—*Kristin Shaw, Castleton, NY*

Prep: 25 min. • **Bake:** 20 min.
Makes: 6 servings

- 2 Tbsp. butter
- 1¼ lbs. beef top sirloin steak, cut into ½-in. cubes
- ¼ tsp. pepper
- 1 pkg. (16 oz.) frozen vegetables for stew
- 2 Tbsp. water
- ½ tsp. dried thyme
- 1 jar (12 oz.) mushroom or beef gravy
- 1 tube (8 oz.) refrigerated crescent rolls

1. Preheat oven to 375°. In a 10-in. cast-iron or other ovenproof skillet, heat butter over medium-high heat. Brown beef in batches; remove from pan. Sprinkle with pepper; keep warm.
2. In same skillet, combine the vegetables, water and thyme; stir in gravy. Bring to a boil. Reduce the heat, simmer, uncovered, until vegetables are thawed. Stir in beef; remove from heat.
3. Unroll crescent dough and separate into 8 triangles. Starting from the wide end of each triangle, roll up a third of the length and place over beef mixture with pointed ends toward the center.
4. Bake, uncovered, until golden brown, 16-18 minutes.
1 serving: 365 cal., 18g fat (6g sat. fat), 67mg chol., 716mg sod., 29g carb. (4g sugars, 1g fiber), 22g pro.

"This was a delicious and satisfying one-pot meal for a weeknight. It's easy to put together since there is little chopping, and the cleanup is a breeze. I cut the meat into bite-sized cubes instead of strips. I highly recommend it."
PAGERD, TASTEOFHOME.COM

STROGANOFF SANDWICHES

STROGANOFF SANDWICHES

This recipe is ideal for game day, either at a tailgate party or at home. I often make the meat mixture ahead of time and add the sour cream just before serving.
—*Susan Graham, Cherokee, IA*

Prep: 10 min. • **Cook:** 30 min.
Makes: 8 servings

- 1½ lbs. ground beef
- 1 medium onion, chopped
- ½ cup sliced fresh mushrooms
- 6 to 8 bacon strips, cooked and crumbled
- 2 garlic cloves, minced
- 2 Tbsp. all-purpose flour
- ½ tsp. salt
- ½ tsp. paprika
- ⅛ tsp. ground nutmeg
- 1 can (10¾ oz.) condensed cream of mushroom soup, undiluted
- 1 cup sour cream
- 8 hamburger buns, split

1. In a large cast-iron or other heavy skillet, cook beef, onion and mushrooms over medium heat until meat is no longer pink; drain. Add bacon and garlic. Combine the flour, salt, paprika and nutmeg; gradually stir into beef mixture until blended.
2. Stir in the soup (mixture will be thick) and heat through. Add sour cream. Cook until heated through, stirring occasionally (do not boil), 3-4 minutes longer. Serve on buns.
Freeze option: Freeze cooled meat mixture in freezer containers. To use, partially thaw in refrigerator overnight. Heat through in a saucepan, stirring occasionally; add water if necessary. Serve on buns.
1 sandwich: 392 cal., 19g fat (9g sat. fat), 67mg chol., 845mg sod., 30g carb. (6g sugars, 2g fiber), 22g pro.

MEAT & PEPPER CORNBREAD

I love that I can create this entire dish in one skillet—such convenience!
—*Rita Carlson, Idaho Falls, ID*

- -

Prep: 15 min. • **Bake:** 20 min.
Makes: 6 servings

- 1   lb. ground beef
- 1   cup chopped green pepper
- 1   cup chopped onion
- 2   cans (8 oz. each) tomato sauce
- 1½ tsp. chili powder
- ½   tsp. salt
- ¼   tsp. pepper
- 1   cup all-purpose flour
- ¾   cup cornmeal
- ¼   cup sugar
- 1   Tbsp. baking powder
- ½   tsp. salt
- 1   large egg, room temperature, beaten
- 1   cup 2% milk
- ¼   cup canola oil

1. In a 10-in. cast-iron or other ovenproof skillet, lightly brown ground beef, green pepper and onion; drain. Add tomato sauce, chili powder, salt and pepper; simmer 10-15 minutes.
2. Meanwhile, combine dry ingredients. Combine egg, milk and oil; stir into dry ingredients just until moistened. Pour over beef mixture.
3. Bake at 400° until golden, 20-25 minutes. Serve in skillet, or cool briefly, then run a knife around edge of skillet and invert on a serving plate; cut into wedges.
1 wedge: 432 cal., 18g fat (5g sat. fat), 87mg chol., 839mg sod., 46g carb. (13g sugars, 3g fiber), 22g pro.

BEEF & SPINACH
SKILLET

BEEF & SPINACH SKILLET

Over the years, I've tried to instill a love of cooking in our children. We've enjoyed a variety of delicious recipes, including this savory, comforting stovetop entree.
—*Nancy Robaidek, Krakow, WI*

- -

Prep: 20 min. • **Cook:** 15 min.
Makes: 6 servings

- 1   lb. ground beef
- 1   medium onion, chopped
- 1   pkg. (10 oz.) frozen chopped spinach, thawed and squeezed dry
- 1   can (4 oz.) mushroom stems and pieces, drained
- 1   tsp. garlic salt
- 1   tsp. dried basil
- ¼   cup butter
- ¼   cup all-purpose flour
- ½   tsp. salt
- 2   cups whole milk
- 1   cup shredded Monterey Jack cheese or part-skim mozzarella cheese
    Biscuits, optional

1. In a 10-in. cast-iron or other ovenproof skillet, cook beef and onion over medium heat until meat is no longer pink; drain. Add the spinach, mushrooms, garlic salt and basil. Cover and cook for 5 minutes.
2. In a saucepan, melt butter over medium heat. Stir in the flour and salt until smooth. Gradually add milk. Bring to a boil; cook and stir until thickened, about 2 minutes. Stir in cheese. Pour over meat mixture; mix well. Reduce heat; cook, covered, until heated through. If desired, serve with biscuits.
1 serving: 351 cal., 23g fat (13g sat. fat), 85mg chol., 872mg sod., 13g carb. (6g sugars, 2g fiber), 23g pro.

TEST KITCHEN TIP
To avoid ending up with lumps in the white sauce, simply stir it with a whisk while it cooks.

TACO SKILLET PIZZA WITH CORNBREAD CRUST

Our family loves taco pizza, and I have made so many versions of it. This recipe is like a deep-dish skillet pizza. It's a hearty meal and can be served straight out of the pan.
—*Pamela Shank, Parkersburg, WV*

- -

Prep: 30 min. • **Bake:** 20 min.
Makes: 6 servings

- ½ lb. lean ground beef (90% lean)
- 1 cup refried beans
- ⅓ cup salsa
- 2 Tbsp. taco seasoning
- 1 pkg. (6 oz.) Mexican-style cornbread/muffin mix
- ⅓ cup tortilla chips, crushed
- 1 cup shredded cheddar cheese
  TOPPINGS: Torn romaine, chopped tomatoes, sour cream, chopped onion, chopped cilantro and fried tortilla strips

1. Preheat oven to 350°. In a 10-in. cast-iron or other ovenproof skillet, cook the beef over medium heat until no longer pink, 6-8 minutes, breaking into crumbles; drain. Transfer to a small bowl. Stir in the beans, salsa and taco seasoning; keep warm. Wipe skillet clean.
2. Prepare cornbread mix according to package directions; stir in crushed tortilla chips. Pour into skillet. Bake 12-15 minutes or until set. Spread ground beef mixture over cornbread to within 1-in. of edges; sprinkle with cheese. Bake until cheese is melted and crust is golden brown, 3-5 minutes. Serve with toppings.
1 wedge: 329 cal., 14g fat (6g sat. fat), 75mg chol., 1052mg sod., 31g carb. (3g sugars, 3g fiber), 19g pro.

MAKEOVER BEEF STROGANOFF

I trimmed the calories, fat and sodium in a classic stroganoff, and my comfy, cozy version still tastes like a Russian masterpiece.
—*Candace Clark, Kelso, WA*

- -

Takes: 30 min. • **Makes:** 6 servings

- ½ cup plus 1 Tbsp. all-purpose flour, divided
- ½ tsp. pepper, divided
- 1 beef top round steak (1½ lbs.), cut into thin strips
- 2 Tbsp. canola oil
- 1 cup sliced fresh mushrooms
- 1 small onion, chopped
- 1 garlic clove, minced
- 1 can (14½ oz.) reduced-sodium beef broth
- ½ tsp. salt
- 1 cup reduced-fat sour cream
  Chopped fresh parsley, optional
  Coarsely ground pepper, optional
- 3 cups cooked yolk-free noodles

1. Combine ½ cup flour and ¼ tsp. pepper in a large bowl. Add beef, a few pieces at a time, and turn to coat.
2. In a large nonstick skillet, heat oil over medium-high heat. Cook beef in batches until no longer pink. Remove and keep warm. In same skillet, saute mushrooms and onion in drippings until tender. Add garlic; cook 1 minute longer.
3. Whisk remaining flour with broth until smooth; stir into skillet. Bring to a boil; cook and stir until thickened, about 2 minutes. Add beef, salt and remaining pepper. Stir in sour cream; heat through (do not boil). If desired, sprinkle with parsley and coarsely ground pepper. Serve with noodles.
1 cup beef stroganoff with ½ cup noodles: 349 cal., 12g fat (4g sat. fat), 78mg chol., 393mg sod., 25g carb. (5g sugars, 2g fiber), 33g pro. **Diabetic exchanges:** 3 lean meat, 2 fat, 1½ starch.

TACO SKILLET PIZZA
WITH CORNBREAD CRUST

SKILLET BOW TIE LASAGNA

This quick recipe tastes just like lasagna, but you make it on the stove. It's very tasty and is always a hit with my family.
—*Arleta Schurle, Clay Center, KS*

Prep: 5 min. • **Cook:** 35 min.
Makes: 4 servings

- 1 lb. ground beef
- 1 small onion, chopped
- 1 garlic clove, minced
- 1 can (14½ oz.) diced tomatoes, undrained
- 1½ cups water
- 1 can (6 oz.) tomato paste
- 1 Tbsp. dried parsley flakes
- 2 tsp. dried oregano
- 1 tsp. salt
- 2½ cups uncooked bow tie pasta
- ¾ cup 4% cottage cheese
- ¼ cup grated Parmesan cheese

1. In a large cast-iron or other heavy skillet, cook beef, onion and garlic until meat is no longer pink; drain. Add the tomatoes, water, tomato paste, parsley, oregano and salt. Stir in the pasta; bring to a boil. Reduce heat; cover and simmer until the pasta is tender, 20-25 minutes, stirring once.
2. Combine cheeses; drop by rounded tablespoonfuls onto pasta mixture. Cover and cook for 5 minutes. If desired, sprinkle with additional dried oregano.
1 cup: 505 cal., 18g fat (7g sat. fat), 77mg chol., 1064mg sod., 52g carb. (11g sugars, 5g fiber), 36g pro.

"This recipe has been a family favorite for years! I like it because it's easy to make and tastes just like oven-baked lasagna."

SGRONHOLZ, TASTEOFHOME.COM

STEAK SANDWICHES WITH QUICK-PICKLED VEGETABLES

This recipe is a Cambodian version of a classic Vietnamese dish. This sandwich has a hint of sour from the pickled vegetables, freshness from the cucumber, spiciness from the Sriracha mayo and sweetness from the marinated beef.
—*Hudson Stiver, Bowen Island, BC*

Prep: 30 min. + marinating
Cook: 15 min. + standing • **Makes:** 6 servings

- 1 cup white vinegar
- 1 Tbsp. sugar
- 1½ cups thinly sliced fresh carrots
- 1 small daikon radish, thinly sliced
- ¼ cup packed brown sugar
- ¼ cup rice vinegar
- ¼ cup soy sauce
- 1 beef top sirloin steak (1¼ lbs.)
- 1 Tbsp. olive oil
- 1 French bread baguette (10½ oz.), halved lengthwise
- ½ cup mayonnaise
- 2 Tbsp. Sriracha chili sauce
- ½ cup thinly sliced English cucumber Fresh cilantro leaves

1. In a large bowl, whisk white vinegar and sugar until sugar is dissolved. Add carrots and radish. Refrigerate at least 2 hours. Meanwhile, in a shallow dish, combine brown sugar, rice vinegar and soy sauce. Add beef and turn to coat. Refrigerate 1 hour, turning once. Drain beef, discarding marinade.
2. In a large cast-iron or other heavy skillet, heat oil over medium-high heat. Cook steak until meat reaches desired doneness (for medium-rare, a thermometer should read 135°; medium, 140°; medium-well, 145°), 7-10 minutes on each side. Let rest for 10 minutes before slicing.
3. Meanwhile, place the baguette on an ungreased baking sheet, cut sides up. Broil 3-4 in. from heat until golden brown, about 3-4 minutes. Drain the carrots and radish, reserving 1½ tsp. vinegar marinade. In a small bowl, combine mayonnaise, chili sauce and reserved vinegar marinade; spread half over cut sides of baguette. Top with steak, cucumber, pickled vegetables and cilantro; replace top. Cut crosswise into 6 slices. Serve with remaining mayonnaise mixture.
1 sandwich: 430 cal., 20g fat (4g sat. fat), 40mg chol., 888mg sod., 37g carb. (9g sugars, 2g fiber), 25g pro.

OVEN SWISS STEAK

OVEN SWISS STEAK

I was really glad to find this recipe since it's a great way to use round steak and it picks up fabulous flavor from one of my favorite herbs—tarragon. I am a homemaker with three children and enjoy cooking tasty dinners like this one for my family.
—Lorna Dickau, Vanderhoof, BC

Prep: 30 min. • **Bake:** 1¼ hours
Makes: 6 servings

- 8   bacon strips
- 2   lbs. beef top round steak (¾ in. thick)
- 2   cups sliced fresh mushrooms
- 1   can (14½ oz.) diced tomatoes, undrained
- ½   cup chopped onion
- 1   to 2 tsp. dried tarragon
- 2   Tbsp. cornstarch
- 2   Tbsp. water
- 1   cup heavy whipping cream
       Minced fresh parsley, optional

1. In a large cast-iron or ovenproof skillet, cook the bacon over medium heat until crisp. Remove to paper towels to drain, reserving ¼ cup drippings. Crumble the bacon and set aside.

2. Trim beef; cut into serving-size pieces. Brown on both sides in drippings. Top meat with mushrooms, tomatoes and onion. Sprinkle with tarragon and bacon. Cover and bake at 325° for 1¼-1¾ hours or until meat is tender, basting twice.

3. Remove meat to a serving platter; keep warm. Combine cornstarch and water until smooth; add to skillet. Bring to a boil; cook and stir 2 minutes or until thickened. Reduce heat; stir in cream. Simmer, uncovered, until heated through, 3-4 minutes. Return meat to skillet and turn to coat with sauce. If desired, sprinkle with parsley.

1 serving: 385 cal., 26g fat (12g sat. fat), 116mg chol., 308mg sod., 7g carb. (4g sugars, 1g fiber), 31g pro.

ROASTED CHICKEN
WITH VEGGIES, PAGE 62

CAST IRON
CHICKEN & TURKEY

When it comes to hearty meals in a hurry, you can't beat poultry.
Loaded with flavor and versatility, chicken and turkey are
convenient, savory staples for today's home cooks.

SKILLET CHICKEN FAJITAS

ENCHILADA CHICKEN

We enjoy southwestern flavors and this easy recipe never gets boring. The chicken sizzles in the skillet before getting baked and comes out tender and juicy every time.
—*Nancy Sousley, Lafayette, IN*

Prep: 15 min. • **Bake:** 20 min.
Makes: 4 servings

- 4   boneless skinless chicken breast halves (6 oz. each)
- 2   tsp. salt-free Southwest chipotle seasoning blend
- 1   Tbsp. olive oil
- ¼   cup enchilada sauce
- ½   cup shredded sharp cheddar cheese
- 2   Tbsp. minced fresh cilantro

Sprinkle chicken with seasoning blend. In an ovenproof skillet, brown chicken in oil. Top with enchilada sauce, cheese and cilantro. Bake at 350° for 18-20 minutes or until a thermometer reads 170°.

1 chicken breast half: 265 cal., 11g fat (5g sat. fat), 109mg chol., 252mg sod., 2g carb. (0 sugars, 0 fiber), 38g pro. **Diabetic exchanges:** 5 lean meat, 1 fat.

MAPLE-DIJON CHICKEN

Eating dinner as a family every night is really important to us, and this entree is one we adore. It's our favorite skillet dish.
—*Courtney Stultz, Weir, KS*

Takes: 30 min. • **Makes:** 4 servings

- 1   lb. boneless skinless chicken breasts, cut into 1-in.-thick strips
- ½   tsp. dried rosemary, crushed
- ½   tsp. dried thyme
- ½   tsp. pepper
- ¼   tsp. salt
- 1   Tbsp. coconut oil or olive oil
- ½   cup chopped onion
- 1   garlic clove, minced
- ⅓   cup Dijon mustard
- 3   Tbsp. maple syrup

Toss chicken with seasonings. In a large skillet, heat oil over medium heat; saute chicken 10 minutes. Add onion and garlic; cook and stir 5 minutes. Stir in the mustard and syrup; cook and stir until the sauce is caramelized and chicken is no longer pink, 5-7 minutes.

1 serving: 221 cal., 6g fat (4g sat. fat), 63mg chol., 684mg sod., 13g carb. (10g sugars, 1g fiber), 23g pro. **Diabetic exchanges:** 3 lean meat, 1 starch, ½ fat.

SKILLET CHICKEN FAJITAS

"Fresh flavor with a flair" describes this quick and easy recipe. Fajitas are just right for hot summer evenings when you want to serve something fun and tasty, yet keep cooking to a minimum. Try topping them with sour cream, guacamole or both. My family just loves them!
—*Lindsay St. John, Plainfield, IN*

Takes: 30 min. • **Makes:** 6 servings

- ¼   cup lime juice
- 1   garlic clove, minced
- 1   tsp. chili powder
- ½   tsp. salt
- ½   tsp. ground cumin
- 2   Tbsp. olive oil, divided
- 1½ lbs. boneless skinless chicken breasts, cut into strips
- 1   medium onion, cut into thin wedges
- ½   medium sweet red pepper, cut into strips
- ½   medium yellow pepper, cut into strips
- ½   medium green pepper, cut into strips
- ½   cup salsa
- 12 flour tortillas (8 in.), warmed
- 1½ cups shredded cheddar cheese or Monterey Jack cheese

1. Mix first 5 ingredients and 1 Tbsp. oil. Add chicken; toss to coat. Let stand 15 minutes.
2. In a large nonstick skillet, heat remaining oil over medium-high heat; saute onion and peppers until crisp-tender, 3-4 minutes. Remove from pan.
3. In same skillet, saute chicken mixture until no longer pink, 3-4 minutes. Stir in salsa and pepper mixture; heat through. Serve in the tortillas. Sprinkle with cheese.

1 fajita: 621 cal., 24g fat (8g sat. fat), 91mg chol., 999mg sod., 61g carb. (3g sugars, 4g fiber), 38g pro.

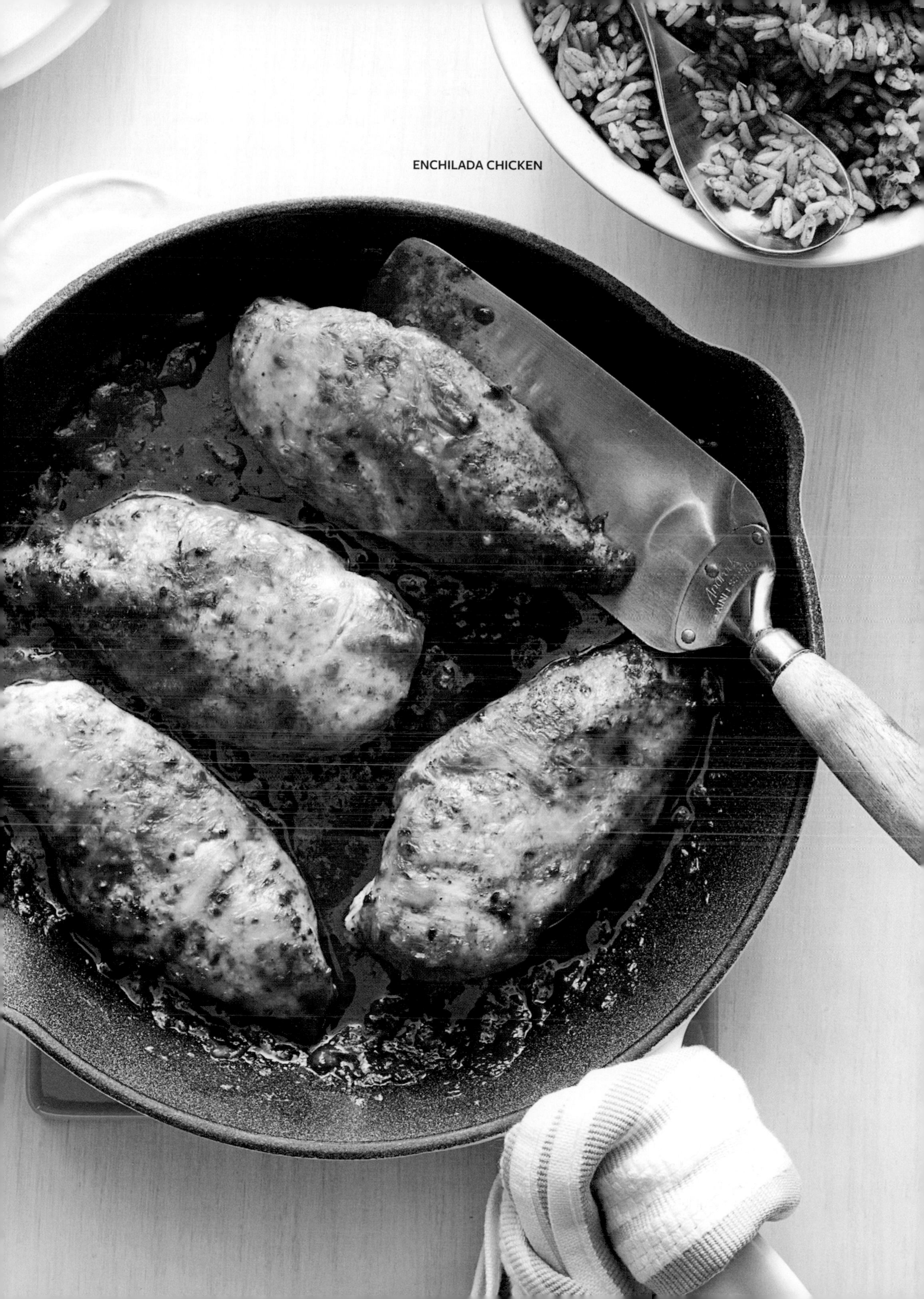

ENCHILADA CHICKEN

TURKEY CURRY

I'm always looking for new and interesting ways to use leftover turkey—especially around the holidays. This is a zesty entree you can make as spicy as you'd like by varying the amount of curry powder.
—*Martha Balser, Cincinnati, OH*

Takes: 20 min. • **Makes:** 4 servings

- 1 cup sliced celery
- ½ cup sliced carrots
- 1 cup fat-free milk
- 2 Tbsp. cornstarch
- ¾ cup reduced-sodium chicken broth
- 2 cups diced cooked turkey or chicken
- 2 Tbsp. dried minced onion
- ½ tsp. garlic powder
- 1 to 4 tsp. curry powder
  Hot cooked rice, optional

1. Lightly coat a skillet with cooking spray; saute celery and carrots until tender. In a bowl, mix ¼ cup milk and cornstarch until smooth. Add broth and remaining milk; mix until smooth.
2. Pour over vegetables. Bring to a boil; cook and stir for 2 minutes or until thickened. Add the turkey, onion, garlic powder and curry powder; heat through, stirring occasionally. Serve with rice if desired.
1 cup: 172 cal., 3g fat (1g sat. fat), 72mg chol., 235mg sod., 12g carb. (5g sugars, 1g fiber), 24g pro. **Diabetic exchanges:** 1 starch, 3 lean meat.

SAUCY MEDITERRANEAN CHICKEN WITH RICE

The hints of Mediterranean flavor in this chicken dish make it a family favorite.
—*Tabitha Alloway, Edna, KS*

Takes: 30 min. • **Makes:** 4 servings

- ¾ cup water
- 3 Tbsp. tomato paste
- 2 Tbsp. lemon juice
- ¾ tsp. salt
- 1 tsp. chili powder
- ½ tsp. garlic powder
- ½ tsp. ground ginger
- ¼ tsp. ground fennel seed
- ¼ tsp. ground turmeric
- 1 tsp. ground coriander, optional
- 3 Tbsp. olive oil
- 1 medium onion, chopped
- 1 lb. boneless skinless chicken breasts, cut into 1-in. cubes
- 3 cups hot cooked rice
  Minced fresh parsley, optional

1. In a small bowl, mix the water, tomato paste, lemon juice, salt, chili powder, garlic powder, ginger, fennel, turmeric and, if desired, coriander until smooth.
2. In a large skillet, heat oil over medium-high heat. Add onions; cook and stir until tender. Stir in chicken; brown 3-4 minutes. Pour water mixture into pan.
3. Bring to a boil. Reduce heat; simmer, uncovered, until chicken is no longer pink, 8-10 minutes. Serve with rice. If desired, top with parsley.
¾ cup chicken mixture with ¾ cup rice: 394 cal., 13g fat (2g sat. fat), 63mg chol., 527mg sod., 40g carb. (3g sugars, 2g fiber), 27g pro. **Diabetic exchanges:** 3 lean meat, 2½ starch, 2 fat.

TEST KITCHEN TIP
Don't have any leftover rice to hurry along this recipe? No problem! Simply make some. Just remember that long grain rice triples when cooked, and instant rice doubles. So you'll need 1 cup uncooked long grain or 1½ cups uncooked instant to yield about 3 cups hot cooked rice.

SAUCY MEDITERRANEAN CHICKEN WITH RICE

CHICKEN & VEGETABLE
CURRY COUSCOUS

ZIPPY TURKEY ZOODLES

Eating healthy doesn't mean sacrificing flavor—and these spiced-up zoodles prove it. If you don't have a spiralizer, simply slice the zucchini julienne-style.
—*Elizabeth Bramkamp, Gig Harbor, WA*

Prep: 25 min. • **Cook:** 20 min.
Makes: 4 servings

    4   tsp. olive oil, divided
    1   lb. ground turkey
    1   small onion, finely chopped
    1   jalapeno pepper,
        seeded and chopped
    2   garlic cloves, minced
    ¾   tsp. ground cumin
    ½   tsp. salt
    ¼   tsp. chili powder
    ¼   tsp. crushed red pepper flakes
    ¼   tsp. pepper
    3   medium zucchini, spiralized
    4   plum tomatoes, chopped
    1   cup frozen corn, thawed
    1   cup black beans, rinsed and drained
        Optional: Chopped fresh cilantro and
        shredded cheddar cheese

1. In a large nonstick skillet, heat 2 tsp. olive oil over medium heat. Add turkey, onion, jalapeno and garlic and cook 8-10 minutes or until turkey is no longer pink and vegetables are tender, breaking up turkey into crumbles; drain. Stir in seasonings; remove and keep warm. Wipe out pan.
2. In the same pan, heat remaining olive oil; cook zucchini over medium heat until crisp-tender, 3-5 minutes. Stir in tomatoes, corn, beans and reserved turkey mixture; heat through. Serve with cilantro and cheese if desired.

1¾ cups: 332 cal., 14g fat (3g sat. fat), 75mg chol., 500mg sod., 26g carb. (7g sugars, 6g fiber), 29g pro. **Diabetic exchanges:** 3 medium-fat meat, 2 vegetable, 1 starch, 1 fat

CHICKEN & VEGETABLE CURRY COUSCOUS

For my busy family, a semi-homemade one-pot meal is the best way to get dinner done in a hurry. Use your favorite blend of frozen veggies and serve with toasted pita bread for smiles all around.
—*Elizabeth Hokanson, Arborg, MB*

Takes: 25 min. • **Makes:** 6 servings

    1   Tbsp. butter
    1   lb. boneless skinless chicken breasts,
        cut into strips
    1   pkg. (16 oz.) frozen
        vegetable blend of your choice
    1¼ cups water
    1   pkg. (5.7 oz.) curry-flavored
        couscous mix
    ½   cup raisins

1. In a cast-iron or other heavy skillet, heat butter over medium-high heat. Add chicken; cook and stir until no longer pink.
2. Add vegetable blend, water and contents of couscous seasoning packet. Bring to a boil; stir in couscous and raisins. Remove from heat; let stand, covered, until water is absorbed, about 5 minutes. Fluff with a fork.

1 cup: 273 cal., 4g fat (2g sat. fat), 47mg chol., 311mg sod., 39g carb. (9g sugars, 4g fiber), 21g pro. **Diabetic exchanges:** 2 starch, 2 lean meat, 1 vegetable, ½ fat.

CHICKEN BURRITO SKILLET

We love Mexican night at our house, and I love to re-create dishes from our favorite restaurants. This burrito-inspired entree is ready for the table in almost no time!
—*Krista Marshall, Fort Wayne, IN*

Prep: 15 min. • **Cook:** 30 min.
Makes: 6 servings

- 1 lb. boneless skinless chicken breasts, cut into 1½-in. pieces
- ⅛ tsp. salt
- ⅛ tsp. pepper
- 2 Tbsp. olive oil, divided
- 1 cup uncooked long grain rice
- 1 can (15 oz.) black beans, rinsed and drained
- 1 can (14½ oz.) diced tomatoes, drained
- 1 tsp. ground cumin
- ½ tsp. onion powder
- ½ tsp. garlic powder
- ½ tsp. chili powder
- 2½ cups reduced-sodium chicken broth
- 1 cup shredded Mexican cheese blend
- 1 medium tomato, chopped
- 3 green onions, chopped

1. Toss chicken with salt and pepper. In a large cast-iron or other heavy skillet, heat 1 Tbsp. oil over medium-high heat; saute chicken until browned, about 2 minutes. Remove from pan.
2. In same pan, heat remaining oil over medium-high heat; saute rice until lightly browned, 1-2 minutes. Stir in beans, canned tomatoes, seasonings and broth; bring to a boil. Place chicken on top (do not stir into rice). Simmer, covered, until rice is tender and chicken is no longer pink, 20-25 minutes.
3. Remove from heat; sprinkle with cheese. Let stand, covered, until cheese is melted. Top with tomato and green onions.

1⅓ cups: 403 cal., 13g fat (4g sat. fat), 58mg chol., 690mg sod., 43g carb. (4g sugars, 5g fiber), 27g pro. **Diabetic exchanges:** 3 starch, 3 lean meat, 1½ fat.

TEST KITCHEN TIP
Any can of beans you have in your pantry will work well in this recipe. Our Test Kitchen staff thought pintos and kidney beans would also work particularly well here.

ROASTED CHICKEN WITH VEGGIES

Thyme flavors this moist, golden brown chicken that's surrounded by bright, tender vegetables for meal-in-one convenience.
—*Mary Beth Hansen, Columbia, TN*

Prep: 20 min. • **Bake:** 1½ hours
Makes: 6 servings

- 1 broiler/fryer chicken (3 to 3½ lbs.)
- 1 Tbsp. canola oil
- ½ tsp. salt, divided
- ½ tsp. pepper, divided
- 6 medium carrots, cut into 1-in. pieces
- 4 celery ribs, cut into 1-in. pieces
- 3 medium baking potatoes, peeled and cut into 1½-in. pieces
- 2 medium onions, cut into wedges
- 2 Tbsp. butter, melted
- 4 tsp. minced fresh thyme or 1 tsp. dried thyme

1. Preheat oven to 375°. Place chicken, breast side up, in a 14-in. cast-iron or other ovenproof skillet. Rub with oil; sprinkle with ¼ tsp. salt and ¼ tsp. pepper. If desired, tie legs together with baker's twine. Bake, uncovered, 1 hour.
2. Arrange the carrots, celery, potatoes and onions around chicken. Combine butter and thyme; drizzle over the chicken and vegetables. Sprinkle with remaining ¼ tsp. salt and ¼ tsp. pepper.
3. Cover and bake until a thermometer inserted in thickest part of thigh reads 170°-175° and vegetables are tender, 30-45 minutes.

¼ pound: 329 cal., 10g fat (3g sat. fat), 80mg chol., 187mg sod., 31g carb. (9g sugars, 5g fiber), 28g pro. **Diabetic exchanges:** 3 lean meat, 2 vegetable, 1½ starch.

READY IN 20 MINS.

CASHEW CHICKEN
WITH NOODLES

CASHEW CHICKEN WITH NOODLES

I tried this recipe with some friends one night when we were doing freezer meals. I was smitten! It's quick, easy and delicious!
—*Anita Beachy, Bealeton, VA*

- -

Takes: 20 min. • **Makes:** 4 servings

- 8 oz. uncooked thick rice noodles
- ¼ cup reduced-sodium soy sauce
- 2 Tbsp. cornstarch
- 3 garlic cloves, minced
- 1 lb. boneless skinless chicken breasts, cubed
- 1 Tbsp. peanut oil
- 1 Tbsp. sesame oil
- 6 green onions, cut into 2-in. pieces
- 1 cup unsalted cashews
- 2 Tbsp. sweet chili sauce
  Toasted sesame seeds, optional

1. Cook rice noodles according to package directions.
2. Meanwhile, in a small bowl, combine the soy sauce, cornstarch and garlic. Add the chicken. In a large cast-iron or other heavy skillet, saute chicken mixture in peanut and sesame oils until no longer pink. Add onions; cook 1 minute longer.
3. Drain noodles; stir into skillet. Add cashews and chili sauce and heat through. If desired, top with toasted sesame seeds.
1½ cups: 638 cal., 26g fat (5g sat. fat), 63mg chol., 870mg sod., 68g carb. (6g sugars, 3g fiber), 33g pro.

"Loved this. I added broccoli and edamame with the onions, and it was very tasty!"

RMBARR059, TASTEOFHOME.COM

CHICKEN
BULGUR SKILLET

CHICKEN BULGUR SKILLET

This recipe was passed on to me by a friend, and I've altered it slightly to suit our tastes. We like it with a fresh green salad.
—*Leann Hillmer, Sylvan Grove, KS*

Prep: 15 min. • **Cook:** 30 min.
Makes: 4 servings

- 1 lb. boneless skinless chicken breasts, cut into 1-in. cubes
- 2 tsp. olive oil
- 2 medium carrots, chopped
- ⅔ cup chopped onion
- 3 Tbsp. chopped walnuts
- ½ tsp. caraway seeds
- ¼ tsp. ground cumin
- 1½ cups bulgur
- 2 cups reduced-sodium chicken broth
- 2 Tbsp. raisins
- ¼ tsp. salt
- ⅛ tsp. ground cinnamon

1. In a large cast-iron or other heavy skillet, cook chicken in oil over medium-high heat until meat is no longer pink. Remove and keep warm. In the same skillet, cook and stir the carrots, onion, nuts, caraway seeds and cumin until the onion starts to brown, 3-4 minutes.

2. Stir in bulgur. Gradually add broth; bring to a boil over medium heat. Reduce heat; add the raisins, salt, cinnamon and chicken. Cover and simmer until the bulgur is tender, 12-15 minutes.

1½ cups: 412 cal., 8g fat (1g sat. fat), 66mg chol., 561mg sod., 51g carb. (8g sugars, 12g fiber), 36g pro.

SPINACH & FETA STUFFED CHICKEN

SPINACH & FETA STUFFED CHICKEN

These savory chicken bundles are simple and comforting. I serve them with wild rice and green beans for one of our favorite meals.
—*Jim Knepper, Mount Holly Springs, PA*

Takes: 30 min. • **Makes:** 2 servings

- 8 oz. fresh spinach (about 10 cups)
- 1½ tsp. cider vinegar
- ½ tsp. sugar
- ⅛ tsp. pepper
- 2 boneless skinless chicken thighs
- ½ tsp. chicken seasoning
- 3 Tbsp. crumbled feta cheese
- 1 tsp. olive oil
- ¾ cup reduced-sodium chicken broth
- 1 tsp. butter

1. Preheat the oven to 375°. In a large skillet, cook and stir spinach over medium-high heat until wilted. Stir in vinegar, sugar and pepper; cool slightly.

2. Pound chicken thighs with a meat mallet to flatten slightly; sprinkle with the chicken seasoning. Top chicken with spinach mixture and cheese. Roll up chicken from a long side; tie securely with kitchen string.

3. In an ovenproof skillet, heat olive oil over medium-high heat; add chicken and brown on all sides. Transfer to oven; roast until a thermometer inserted in chicken reads 170°, 13-15 minutes.

4. Remove chicken from pan; keep warm. On stovetop, add broth and butter to skillet; bring to a boil, stirring to loosen browned bits from pan. Cook until slightly thickened, 3-5 minutes. Serve with chicken.

1 chicken roll-up with 2 Tbsp. sauce: 253 cal., 14g fat (5g sat. fat), 86mg chol., 601mg sod., 5g carb. (2g sugars, 2g fiber), 26g pro. **Diabetic exchanges:** 3 lean meat, 2 vegetable, 1½ fat.

CHICKEN FLORENTINE PANINI

This grilled sandwich combines chicken with provolone cheese, spinach and red onion.
—*Lee Bremson, Kansas City, MO*

Takes: 25 min. • **Makes:** 4 servings

- 1 pkg. (5 oz.) fresh baby spinach
- 2 tsp. olive oil
- ¼ cup butter, softened
- 8 slices sourdough bread
- ¼ cup creamy Italian salad dressing
- 8 slices provolone cheese
- ½ lb. shaved deli chicken
- 2 slices red onion, separated into rings

1. In a large cast-iron or other heavy skillet, saute spinach in oil for 2 minutes or until wilted. Drain; wipe skillet clean.
2. Spread 4 bread slices with salad dressing. Layer with a cheese slice, chicken, spinach, onion and another cheese slice. Top with the remaining bread. Butter outsides of the sandwiches.
3. Cook in same skillet or panini maker until bread is golden brown and cheese is melted.
1 sandwich: 582 cal., 26g fat (10g sat. fat), 62mg chol., 1688mg sod., 63g carb. (4g sugars, 5g fiber), 23g pro.

BARBECUED STRAWBERRY CHICKEN

A TASTE OF SUMMER

BARBECUED STRAWBERRY CHICKEN

When it's time to impress family and friends, we serve barbecued chicken garnished with strawberries. It's easier than anyone would ever guess.
—*Bonnie Hawkins, Elkhorn, WI*

Prep: 25 min. • **Bake:** 15 min.
Makes: 4 servings

- 2 Tbsp. canola oil
- 4 boneless skinless chicken breast halves (6 oz. each)
- 2 Tbsp. butter
- ¼ cup finely chopped red onion
- 1 cup barbecue sauce
- 2 Tbsp. brown sugar
- 2 Tbsp. balsamic vinegar
- 2 Tbsp. honey
- 1 cup sliced fresh strawberries

1. Preheat oven to 350°. In a large ovenproof skillet, heat the oil over medium-high heat. Brown chicken on both sides. Remove from pan. In same pan, heat butter over medium-high heat. Add onion; cook and stir until tender, about 1 minute.
2. Stir in barbecue sauce, brown sugar, vinegar and honey. Bring to a boil. Reduce heat; simmer, uncovered, until thickened, 4-6 minutes. Return the chicken to pan. Bake until a thermometer reads 165°, 12-15 minutes. Stir in strawberries.
1 chicken breast half with ⅓ cup sauce: 495 cal., 17g fat (5g sat. fat), 109mg chol., 829mg sod., 49g carb. (42g sugars, 2g fiber), 35g pro.

TURKEY BISCUIT SKILLET

My mother made this while we were growing up, and now I prepare it for my own family. I use the smaller biscuits because they brown up so nicely on top. I also add mushrooms to this recipe sometimes because my family just loves them.
—Keri Boffeli, Monticello, IA

- -

Takes: 30 min. • **Makes:** 6 servings

- 1 Tbsp. butter
- ⅓ cup chopped onion
- ¼ cup all-purpose flour
- 1 can (10½ oz.) condensed chicken broth, undiluted
- ¼ cup fat-free milk
- ⅛ tsp. pepper
- 2 cups cubed cooked turkey breast
- 2 cups frozen peas and carrots (about 10 oz.), thawed
- 1 tube (12 oz.) refrigerated buttermilk biscuits, quartered

1. Preheat oven to 400°. Melt butter in a 10-in. cast-iron or other ovenproof skillet over medium-high heat. Add onion; cook and stir until tender, 2-3 minutes.
2. In a small bowl, mix flour, broth, milk and pepper until smooth; stir into pan. Bring to a boil, stirring constantly; cook and stir until thickened, 1-2 minutes. Add the turkey and frozen vegetables; heat through. Arrange biscuits over stew. Bake until biscuits are golden brown, 15-20 minutes.
1 serving: 319 cal., 10g fat (4g sat. fat), 43mg chol., 878mg sod., 36g carb. (4g sugars, 2g fiber), 22g pro.

TURKEY BISCUIT SKILLET

CHICKEN PESTO MEATBALLS

These tender, pesto-flavored meatballs get gobbled up in our house. They're short on ingredients, but packed with taste. I always make a double batch, freezing the other half for a busy night.
—Ally Billhorn, Wilton, IA

- -

Takes: 30 min. • **Makes:** 4 servings

- 6 oz. uncooked whole grain spaghetti
- ¼ cup dry bread crumbs
- 2 Tbsp. prepared pesto
- 2 Tbsp. grated Parmesan cheese
- 1 tsp. garlic powder
- 1 lb. lean ground chicken
- 1½ cups marinara sauce
- ¼ cup water
  Optional: Torn fresh basil and additional Parmesan cheese

1. Cook spaghetti according to package directions; drain.
2. In a large bowl, combine bread crumbs, pesto, cheese and garlic powder. Add the chicken; mix lightly but thoroughly. Shape into 1-in. balls.
3. In a large skillet, brown meatballs over medium heat, turning occasionally. Add sauce and water; bring to a boil. Reduce heat; simmer, covered, until meatballs are cooked through, about 5 minutes. Serve with spaghetti. If desired, top with basil and additional cheese.
Freeze option: Freeze cooled meatball mixture in freezer containers. To use, partially thaw in refrigerator overnight. Heat through in a covered saucepan over low heat, stirring gently; add water if necessary.
¾ cup meatball mixture with 1 cup spaghetti: 422 cal., 12g fat (3g sat. fat), 85mg chol., 706mg sod., 45g carb. (7g sugars, 7g fiber), 32g pro. **Diabetic exchanges:** 3 starch, 3 lean meat, 1½ fat.

ONE-SKILLET PASTA

This recipe was given to me 25 years ago and remains a family favorite. It's a simple dish with a great twist on traditional spaghetti. Cooking everything in one pot saves time on prep and cleanup.
—*Susan Spence, Lawrenceville, VA*

- -

Prep: 20 min. • **Cook:** 1¼ hours
Makes: 5 servings

- 1½ lbs. ground turkey
- 1 medium onion, finely chopped
- 1 medium sweet red pepper, finely chopped
- 1 can (28 oz.) diced tomatoes, undrained
- 1 can (14½ oz.) fire-roasted diced tomatoes, undrained
- 1 can (14½ oz.) reduced-sodium beef broth
- 1 can (4 oz.) sliced mushrooms, drained
- 1 Tbsp. packed brown sugar
- 1 Tbsp. chili powder
- 8 oz. uncooked angel hair pasta
- 1 cup shredded cheddar cheese

1. In a large cast-iron or other heavy skillet, cook the turkey, onion and pepper over medium heat until turkey is no longer pink; drain.
2. Add the tomatoes, broth, mushrooms, brown sugar and chili powder. Bring to a boil. Reduce heat; simmer, uncovered, for 30 minutes.
3. Add pasta; return to a boil. Reduce heat; cover and simmer 30-35 minutes or until pasta is tender. Sprinkle with cheese. Cover and cook 2-3 minutes longer or until cheese is melted.

1⅔ cups: equals 621 cal., 28 g fat (11 g sat. fat), 118 mg chol., 967 mg sod., 58 g carb., 7 g fiber, 36 g pro.

TEST KITCHEN TIP

Guess what? You can freeze this tasty dish for busy nights. Transfer individual portions of cooled pasta to freezer containers and freeze for up to 3 months. To use, partially thaw in refrigerator overnight. Heat through in a saucepan, stirring occasionally; add broth if necessary.

ONE-SKILLET PASTA

ASIAN TURKEY BURGER WITH APPLE SLAW

I wanted to amp up the flavor of the turkey burgers I made at home. On a whim, I added hoisin sauce, gingerroot and garlic. Now we enjoy these about once a week.
—*Ashley Gayle, Ellicott City, MD*

Takes: 30 min. • **Makes:** 4 servings

- 3 green onions, finely chopped
- 2 Tbsp. hoisin sauce
- 1 Tbsp. minced fresh gingerroot
- 2 garlic cloves, minced
- ½ tsp. salt
- ¼ tsp. pepper
- 1¼ lbs. ground turkey
- 1 Tbsp. olive oil

SLAW
- 3 Tbsp. olive oil
- 1 Tbsp. cider vinegar
- 1 tsp. Dijon mustard
- ¼ tsp. salt
- ⅛ tsp. pepper
- 2 medium apples, julienned
- 2 green onions, finely chopped

ASSEMBLY
- 4 hamburger buns, split and toasted
- 2 Tbsp. hoisin sauce

1. In a large bowl, mix green onions, hoisin sauce, ginger, garlic, salt and pepper. Add turkey; mix lightly but thoroughly. Shape into four ¾-in.-thick patties.
2. In a large cast-iron or other heavy skillet, heat oil over medium heat. Cook burgers until a thermometer reads 165°, 7-9 minutes on each side.
3. Meanwhile, for slaw, in a large bowl, whisk oil, vinegar, mustard, salt and pepper. Add the apples and green onions, toss to coat. To assemble, spread bun bottoms with hoisin sauce. Top with burgers and slaw; replace the tops.
Freeze option: Place patties on a plastic wrap-lined baking sheet; wrap and freeze until firm. Remove from the pan and transfer to a freezer container; return to freezer. To use frozen patties, cook patties as directed, increasing the cooking time as necessary for a thermometer to read 165°.
1 burger with 1 cup apple slaw: 526 cal., 26g fat (5g sat. fat), 94mg chol., 1024mg sod., 41g carb. (15g sugars, 4g fiber), 33g pro.

ONE-POT CHICKEN PESTO PASTA

When my garden basil goes nuts, I make pesto and keep it frozen in small containers for the right opportunity, like this saucy one-pot chicken with pasta.
—*Kimberly Fenwick, Hobart, IN*

Takes: 30 min. • **Makes:** 4 servings

- 1 lb. boneless skinless chicken thighs, cut into 1-in. pieces
- 1 tsp. salt-free seasoning blend
- 2 tsp. olive oil
- 1 can (14½ oz.) reduced-sodium chicken broth
- 2 Tbsp. lemon juice
- 1 cup uncooked gemelli or spiral pasta
- 2 cups fresh broccoli florets
- 1 cup frozen peas
- ⅓ cup prepared pesto

1. Toss chicken with seasoning blend. In a large nonstick skillet, heat oil over medium-high heat. Add chicken and brown evenly; remove from pan.
2. In same pan, combine broth and lemon juice; bring to a boil, stirring to loosen the browned bits from pan. Stir in pasta; return to a boil. Reduce heat; simmer, covered, 10 minutes.
3. Add broccoli; cook, covered, 5 minutes. Return chicken to pan; cook, covered, until pasta is tender and chicken is no longer pink, 2-3 minutes longer, stirring occasionally. Add peas; heat through. Stir in pesto.
1 cup: 404 cal., 18g fat (4g sat. fat), 76mg chol., 646mg sod., 29g carb. (4g sugars, 4g fiber), 30g pro. **Diabetic exchanges:** 3 lean meat, 2 starch, 2 fat.

GLAZED SMOKED
CHOPS WITH
PEARS, PAGE 77

CAST IRON
PORK, HAM & SAUSAGE

Turn here for hearty all-American staples featuring everyone's favorite ingredients. Quick, easy and satisfying, these are the entrees you'll rely on time and again.

**SPICY PORK
TENDERLOIN SALAD**

TORTELLINI WITH SAUSAGE & MASCARPONE

When I crave Italian comfort food on a busy night and don't have a lot of time to cook, this dish is fast and yummy. You can have it on the table in less time than a takeout order.
—*Gerry Vance, Millbrae, CA*

Takes: 20 min. • **Makes:** 6 servings

- 1 pkg. (20 oz.) refrigerated cheese tortellini
- 8 oz. bulk Italian sausage
- 1 jar (24 oz.) pasta sauce with mushrooms
- ½ cup shredded Parmesan cheese
- 1 carton (8 oz.) mascarpone cheese
  Crushed red pepper flakes, optional

1. Prepare tortellini according to package directions. Meanwhile, in a large cast-iron or other heavy skillet, cook sausage over medium heat 6-8 minutes or until no longer pink, breaking into crumbles; drain. Stir in pasta sauce; heat through.
2. Drain tortellini, reserving 1 cup cooking water. Add tortellini to sauce and enough reserved cooking water to reach desired consistency; toss to coat. Stir in Parmesan cheese; dollop with mascarpone cheese. If desired, sprinkle with red pepper flakes.
1 cup: 637 cal., 37g fat (17g sat. fat), 113mg chol., 1040mg sod., 57g carb. (11g sugars, 4g fiber), 24g pro.

"Great weekday meal. It fills all the criteria: quick, easy and tasty."
BLUFFTONNATIVE, TASTEOFHOME.COM

SPICY PORK TENDERLOIN SALAD

A friend served this flavorful salad at a luncheon, and I adjusted it to fit our tastes. Since it's a meal in one, it's perfect for weeknights. And the pretty presentation makes it great for entertaining.
—*Pat Sellon, Monticello, WI*

Prep: 30 min. • **Bake:** 25 min.
Makes: 4 servings

- 4½ tsp. lime juice
- 1½ tsp. orange juice
- 1½ tsp. Dijon mustard
- ½ tsp. curry powder
- ¼ tsp. salt
- ⅛ tsp. pepper
- 2 Tbsp. olive oil
SPICE RUB
- ½ tsp. salt
- ½ tsp. ground cumin
- ½ tsp. ground cinnamon
- ½ tsp. chili powder
- ¼ tsp. pepper
- 1 pork tenderloin (1 lb.)
- 2 tsp. olive oil
- ⅓ cup packed brown sugar
- 6 garlic cloves, minced
- 1½ tsp. hot pepper sauce
- 1 pkg. (6 oz.) fresh baby spinach

1. In a small bowl, whisk first 6 ingredients; gradually whisk in oil. Cover and refrigerate vinaigrette. Combine salt, cumin, cinnamon, chili powder and pepper; rub over meat.
2. In a cast-iron or other ovenproof skillet, brown the meat on all sides in oil, about 8 minutes. Combine the brown sugar, garlic and hot pepper sauce; spread over meat.
3. Bake at 350°, until a thermometer inserted in pork reads 145°, 25-35 minutes. Let stand for 5 minutes before slicing.
4. Toss spinach with vinaigrette. Arrange spinach on serving platter; top with sliced pork. If desired, drizzle with pan juices.
1 serving: 306 cal., 13g fat (3g sat. fat), 64mg chol., 594mg sod., 22g carb. (18g sugars, 2g fiber), 24g pro. **Diabetic exchanges:** 3 lean meat, 2 fat, 1 starch, 1 vegetable.

READY IN 20 MINS.

TORTELLINI
WITH SAUSAGE
& MASCARPONE

ONE-SKILLET PORK CHOP SUPPER

My husband and I reserve this recipe for Sundays after the grandkids have gone home and we're too tired to prepare a big meal. It's comforting and fast.
—*Kathy Thompson, Port Orange, FL*

- -

Prep: 10 min. • **Cook:** 30 min.
Makes: 4 servings

- 1   Tbsp. butter
- 4   pork loin chops
     (½ in. thick and 7 oz. each)
- 3   medium red potatoes,
     cut into small wedges
- 3   medium carrots, cut into ½-in. slices,
     or 2 cups fresh baby carrots
- 1   medium onion, cut into wedges
- 1   can (10¾ oz.) condensed cream
     of mushroom soup, undiluted
- ¼   cup water
     Optional: Cracked black pepper
     and chopped fresh parsley

1. In a large cast-iron or other heavy skillet, heat butter over medium heat. Brown pork chops on both sides; remove from pan, reserving drippings.
2. In same pan, saute vegetables in drippings until lightly browned. Whisk together soup and water; stir into vegetables. Bring to a boil. Reduce heat; simmer, covered, just until vegetables are tender, 15-20 minutes.
3. Add chops; cook, covered, until a thermometer inserted in pork reads 145°. Remove from heat; let stand 5 minutes. If desired, sprinkle with pepper and parsley.
1 serving: 390 cal., 15g fat (6g sat. fat), 97mg chol., 700mg sod., 28g carb. (6g sugars, 4g fiber), 33g pro.

CALZONE ROLLS

CALZONE ROLLS

Big pizza flavor comes through in these rolls. My recipe makes two pans because you'll need 'em! It's so easy to make the dough in the bread machine.
—*Barb Downie, Peterborough, ON*

- -

Prep: 20 min. + rising • **Bake:** 20 min.
Makes: 2 dozen

- 1⅔ cups water (70° to 80°)
- 2   Tbsp. nonfat dry milk powder
- 2   Tbsp. sugar
- 2   Tbsp. shortening
- 1¼ tsp. salt
- 4½ cups all-purpose flour
- 2¼ tsp. active dry yeast
- ½   cup chopped onion
- ½   cup sliced fresh mushrooms
- ½   cup chopped green pepper
- ½   cup chopped sweet red pepper
- 1   Tbsp. olive oil
- ⅓   cup pizza sauce
- ½   cup diced pepperoni
- 1   cup shredded pizza cheese blend
- ¼   cup chopped ripe olives
- 2   Tbsp. grated Parmesan cheese

1. In bread machine pan, place the first 7 ingredients in order suggested by the manufacturer. Select dough setting (check the dough after 5 minutes of mixing; add 1-2 Tbsp. water or flour if needed).
2. In a small skillet, saute onion, mushrooms and peppers in oil until tender; cool.
3. When bread machine cycle is completed, turn dough onto a lightly floured surface; divide in half. Let rest for 5 minutes. Roll each portion into a 16x10-in. rectangle; spread with pizza sauce. Top with the onion mixture, pepperoni, pizza cheese and olives. Roll up each rectangle jelly-roll style, starting with a long side; pinch seam to seal. Cut each into 12 slices (discard end pieces).
4. Place slices cut side down in 2 greased 10-in. cast-iron skillets or 9-in. round baking pans. Sprinkle with Parmesan cheese. Cover and let rise until doubled, about 30 minutes.
5. Bake at 375° 20-30 minutes or until golden brown. Serve warm.
1 roll: 144 cal., 5g fat (2g sat. fat), 7mg chol., 244mg sod., 21g carb. (2g sugars, 1g fiber), 5g pro.

SPICY SAUSAGE & RICE SKILLET

The spicy sausage in this quick skillet dish gives it a kick, and the sliced apples are a pleasant, tart surprise.
—Jamie Jones, Madison, GA

Takes: 30 min. • **Makes:** 6 servings

- 1 pkg. (12 oz.) fully cooked spicy chicken sausage links, halved lengthwise and cut into ½-in. slices
- 1 Tbsp. olive oil
- 2 medium yellow summer squash, chopped
- 2 medium zucchini, chopped
- 1 large sweet red pepper, chopped
- 1 medium onion, chopped
- 1 medium tart apple, cut into ¼-in. slices
- 1 garlic clove, minced
- ½ tsp. salt
- 1 pkg. (8.80 oz.) ready-to-serve brown rice
- 1 can (15 oz.) black beans, rinsed and drained
- ¼ to ½ cup water

1. In a large nonstick skillet, cook sausage over medium-high heat, turning occasionally, until lightly browned. Remove from skillet.
2. In the same skillet, heat oil over medium-high heat. Saute squash, zucchini, pepper, onion, apple, garlic and salt until vegetables are tender, 5-7 minutes. Add the rice, beans, ¼ cup water and sausage; cook and stir until heated through, about 5 minutes, adding more water if needed.
1⅓ cups: 285 cal., 8g fat (2g sat. fat), 43mg chol., 668mg sod., 34g carb. (9g sugars, 6g fiber), 17g pro. **Diabetic exchanges:** 2 starch, 2 lean meat, 1 vegetable, ½ fat.

TEST KITCHEN TIP
To make a meatless version, simply skip the sausage and add more beans.

SPICY SAUSAGE & RICE SKILLET

PRETTY PENNE HAM SKILLET

I'm a busy nurse, so fast meals are a must. This pasta is a tasty change of pace from potato-ham casseroles.
—Kathy Stephan, West Seneca, NY

Takes: 30 min. • **Makes:** 6 servings

- 1 pkg. (16 oz.) penne pasta
- ¼ cup olive oil
- 3 Tbsp. butter
- 3 cups cubed fully cooked ham
- 1 large sweet red pepper, finely chopped
- 1 medium onion, chopped
- 2 garlic cloves, minced
- ¼ cup minced fresh parsley
- 1½ tsp. minced fresh basil or ½ tsp. dried basil
- 1½ tsp. minced fresh oregano or ½ tsp. dried oregano
- 1 can (14½ oz.) chicken broth
- 1 Tbsp. lemon juice
- ½ cup shredded Parmesan cheese

1. Cook the pasta according to package directions; drain. Meanwhile, in a large skillet, heat oil and butter over medium-high heat. Add ham, red pepper and onion; cook and stir 4-6 minutes or until ham is browned and vegetables are tender. Add garlic and herbs; cook 1-2 minutes longer.
2. Stir in broth and lemon juice. Bring to a boil. Reduce heat; simmer, uncovered, until liquid is reduced by half, 10-15 minutes. Add pasta; toss to combine. Sprinkle with cheese.
1⅔ cups: 567 cal., 24g fat (8g sat. fat), 57mg chol., 1344mg sod., 62g carb. (5g sugars, 4g fiber), 27g pro.

SAUSAGE & VEGETABLE SKILLET DINNER

I threw this together one night to use up produce before going out of town. Who knew it was going to be such a hit? Now it's a recipe I turn to whenever time is tight.
—*Elizabeth Kelley, Chicago, IL*

- -

Takes: 30 min. • **Makes:** 4 servings

- 1 Tbsp. olive oil
- 1 pkg. (12 oz.) fully cooked Italian chicken sausage links, cut into 1-in. pieces
- 1 large onion, chopped
- 3 garlic cloves, minced
- ¼ tsp. crushed red pepper flakes
- 1½ lbs. red potatoes (about 5 medium), thinly sliced
- 1 pkg. (10 oz.) frozen corn
- ¼ tsp. pepper
- 1¼ cups vegetable broth
- 2 cups fresh baby spinach

1. In a 12-in. skillet, heat oil over medium-high heat; saute sausage and onion until onion is tender. Add garlic and pepper flakes; cook and stir 1 minute.

2. Add potatoes, corn, pepper and broth; bring to a boil. Reduce heat to medium; cook, covered, until potatoes are tender, 15-20 minutes. Stir in spinach until wilted.

1½ cups: 371 cal., 11g fat (3g sat. fat), 65mg chol., 715mg sod., 48g carb. (6g sugars, 5g fiber), 22g pro. **Diabetic exchanges:** 3 starch, 3 lean meat, 1 fat.

TEST KITCHEN TIP

Italian chicken sausage has less than half the fat of regular. It's lean, but it adds a lot of flavor.

SAUSAGE & VEGETABLE SKILLET DINNER

DEEP-DISH SAUSAGE PIZZA

My grandma made the tastiest snacks for us when we stayed the night at her farm. Her wonderful pizza, hot from the oven, was covered with cheese and had fragrant herb in the crust. Now this pizza is frequently a meal for my husband and me and our two young daughters.
—*Michele Madden,*
Washington Court House, OH

Prep: 30 min. + rising
Bake: 30 min. + standing • **Makes:** 8 se

- 1 pkg. (¼ oz.) active dry yeast
- ⅔ cup warm water (110° to 115°)
- 1¾ to 2 cups all-purpose flour
- ¼ cup vegetable oil
- 1 tsp. each dried oregano, basil and marjoram
- ½ tsp. garlic salt
- ½ tsp. onion salt

TOPPINGS

- 4 cups shredded part-skim mozzarella cheese, divided
- 2 medium green peppers, chopped
- 1 large onion, chopped
- ½ tsp. each dried oregano, basil and marjoram
- 1 Tbsp. olive oil
- 1 cup grated Parmesan cheese
- 1 lb. bulk pork sausage, cooked and drained
- 1 can (28 oz.) diced tomatoes, well drained
- 2 oz. sliced pepperoni

1. In a large bowl, dissolve the yeast in warm water. Add 1 cup flour, oil and crust seasonings; beat until smooth. Add enough remaining flour to form a soft dough.
2. Turn onto a floured surface; knead until smooth and elastic, 6-8 minutes. Place in a greased bowl; turn once to grease top. Cover and let rise in a warm place until doubled, about 1 hour.
3. Punch dough down; roll out into a 15-in. circle. Transfer to a well-greased 12-in. cast-iron, heavy ovenproof skillet or round baking pan, letting crust drape over edges. Sprinkle with 1 cup mozzarella.
4. In another skillet, saute the green peppers, onion and topping seasonings in oil until tender; drain. Layer half of the mixture over crust. Layer with half of the Parmesan, sausage and tomatoes. Sprinkle with 2 cups mozzarella. Repeat layers. Fold crust over to form an edge.

Takes: 30 min. • **Makes:**

- 4 smoked boneless pork chops
- 1 Tbsp. olive oil
- 1 large sweet onion, cut into thin wedges
- ½ cup dry red wine or reduced-sodium chicken broth
- 2 Tbsp. balsamic vinegar
- 2 Tbsp. honey
- 2 large ripe pears, cut into 1-in. wedges

1. Preheat oven to 350°. In a cast-iron or ovenproof skillet over medium-high heat, brown pork chops on both sides; remove from pan.
2. In same pan, heat oil over medium heat; saute onion until tender, 3-5 minutes. Add wine, vinegar and honey; bring to a boil, stirring to loosen any browned bits from pan. Reduce the heat; simmer, uncovered, until slightly thickened, about 5 minutes, stirring occasionally.
3. Return chops to pan; top with pears. Transfer to oven; bake until pears are tender, 10-15 minutes.
1 serving: 313 cal., 4g fat (6g sat. fat), 41mg chol., 1056mg sod., 34g carb. (26g sugars, 4g fiber), 22g pro.

BACON MAC & CHEESE
CORNBREAD SKILLET

BACON MAC & CHEESE CORNBREAD SKILLET

My cast-iron skillet is a workhorse in my kitchen. I just love it for cooking and baking. And this cast-iron mac and cheese recipe can be served as a main dish or cheesy side.
—*Lisa Keys, Kennett Square, PA*

- -

Prep: 35 min. • **Bake:** 30 min. + standing
Makes: 8 servings

1¾ cups uncooked elbow macaroni
8 bacon strips, chopped
1 cup shredded smoked Gouda or cheddar cheese
1 cup shredded pepper jack cheese
4 oz. cream cheese, cubed
6 large eggs, divided use
3 cups 2% milk, divided
4 green onions, chopped
1 tsp. kosher salt, divided
½ tsp. pepper, divided
1 pkg. (8½ oz.) cornbread/muffin mix
½ tsp. smoked paprika
Additional green onions

1. Preheat oven to 400°. Cook macaroni according to package directions. Meanwhile, in a 12-in. cast-iron or other ovenproof skillet, cook bacon over medium heat until crisp, stirring occasionally. Remove with a slotted spoon; drain on paper towels. Discard drippings, reserving 1 Tbsp. in pan.
2. Drain macaroni; add macaroni to drippings. Stir in shredded cheeses and cream cheese; cook and stir over medium heat until cheese is melted, 2-3 minutes. Whisk 2 eggs, 1 cup milk, green onions, ½ tsp. kosher salt and ¼ tsp. pepper; pour into skillet. Cook and stir until slightly thickened, 3-4 minutes. Remove from heat.
3. Reserve ¼ cup bacon for topping; sprinkle remaining bacon over macaroni. Place the cornbread mix, paprika, remaining 4 eggs, 2 cups milk, ½ tsp. kosher salt and ¼ tsp. pepper in a blender; cover and process until smooth. Pour over bacon.
4. Bake until puffed and golden brown, 30-35 minutes. Let stand 10 minutes before serving. Sprinkle with reserved ¼ cup bacon and additional green onions.
1 cup: 497 cal., 27g fat (13g sat. fat), 203mg chol., 978mg sod., 40g carb. (12g sugars, 3g fiber), 23g pro.

QUICK GINGER PORK

QUICK GINGER PORK

My husband and I are empty nesters. It was a challenge learning to cook for just two again, but I've found recipes like this one that give us delicious scaled-down dinners.
—*Esther Johnson Danielson, Lawton, PA*

- -

Takes: 20 min. • **Makes:** 2 servings

½ lb. pork tenderloin, cut into thin strips
1 Tbsp. canola oil
1 garlic clove, minced
2 Tbsp. reduced-sodium soy sauce
¼ tsp. sugar
⅛ to ¼ tsp. ground ginger
½ cup cold water
1½ tsp. cornstarch
Hot cooked rice, optional
Optional: Thinly sliced green onions and toasted sesame seeds

1. In a large skillet or wok, stir-fry the pork in oil until no longer pink. Add the garlic; cook 1 minute longer.
2. In a small bowl, combine the soy sauce, sugar and ginger; add to skillet. Combine water and cornstarch until smooth; add to skillet. Bring to a boil; cook and stir until thickened, about 2 minutes. If desired, serve with rice and top with green onions and sesame seeds.
1 serving: 216 cal., 11g fat (2g sat. fat), 64mg chol., 621mg sod., 4g carb. (1g sugars, 0 fiber), 24g pro. **Diabetic exchanges:** 3 lean meat, 1½ fat, ½ starch.

TEST KITCHEN TIP
Cuts of pork with loin in the name are lean—pork tenderloin, pork loin roast and pork loin chops.

TOUCHDOWN
BRAT SLIDERS

It's game time when these minis make an appearance. Two things my husband loves—beer and brats—get stepped up a notch with crunchy flavored chips.
—*Kirsten Shabaz, Lakeville, MN*

- -

Takes: 50 min. • **Makes:** 16 sliders

5	thick-sliced bacon strips, chopped
1	lb. uncooked bratwurst links, casings removed
1	large onion, finely chopped
2	garlic cloves, minced
1	pkg. (8 oz.) cream cheese, cubed
1	cup dark beer or nonalcoholic beer
1	Tbsp. Dijon mustard
¼	tsp. pepper
16	dinner rolls, split and toasted
2	cups cheddar and sour cream potato chips, crushed

1. In a large cast-iron or other heavy skillet, cook bacon over medium heat until crisp. Remove to paper towels with a slotted spoon; drain, reserving drippings. Cook bratwurst and onion in drippings over medium heat until meat is no longer pink, breaking into crumbles. Add garlic; cook 1 minute longer. Drain well.
2. Stir in the cream cheese, beer, mustard and pepper. Bring to a boil. Reduce heat; simmer, uncovered, 15-20 minutes or until thickened, stirring occasionally. Stir in bacon. Spoon ¼ cup onto each roll; sprinkle with chips. Replace tops.
1 slider: 354 cal., 24g fat (10g sat. fat), 62mg chol., 617mg sod., 23g carb. (2g sugars, 2g fiber), 10g pro.

APPLES & ONION
TOPPED CHOPS

Now that my husband and I are trying to lose weight, I find it a challenge to come up with healthy dishes that are flavorful, quick and appealing to us and our young daughter. This one fits the bill on all counts.
—*Beverly McLain, Endicott, NY*

- -

Takes: 30 min. • **Makes:** 4 servings

4	tsp. canola oil, divided
4	boneless pork loin chops (5 oz. each)
3	cups sweet onion slices
2	medium Granny Smith apples, peeled and sliced
½	cup water
2	Tbsp. brown sugar
1	Tbsp. cider vinegar
1	tsp. garlic powder
½	tsp. salt
¼	to ½ tsp. pepper
¼	tsp. dried rosemary, crushed

1. In a large nonstick skillet heat 2 tsp. canola oil over medium-high heat; cook chops until browned, about 3 minutes on each side. Remove the meat; set aside and keep warm.
2. In same skillet, cook and stir onion in remaining 2 tsp. canola oil for 7 minutes or until golden brown. Add apple slices; cook and stir 3 minutes longer.
3. Combine the water, brown sugar, vinegar, garlic powder, salt, pepper and rosemary. Stir into skillet. Bring to a boil. Return the meat to pan. Reduce heat; cover and cook until the apples are crisp-tender, and a thermometer inserted into chops reads 160°, 8-10 minutes.
1 serving: 326 cal., 13g fat (3g sat. fat), 68mg chol., 340mg sod., 24g carb. (17g sugars, 3g fiber), 28g pro. **Diabetic exchanges:** 4 lean meat, 1 vegetable, 1 fat, ½ starch, ½ fruit

APPLES & ONION
TOPPED CHOPS

KIELBASA
CABBAGE SKILLET

ITALIAN SAUSAGE
VEGGIE SKILLET

We love Italian sausage sandwiches, but because the bread isn't diet-friendly for me, I created this recipe to satisfy my craving. If you like some heat, use hot peppers in place of the sweet peppers.
—Tina Howells, Salem, OH

- -

Takes: 30 min. • **Makes:** 6 servings

- 4 cups uncooked whole wheat spiral pasta
- 1 lb. Italian turkey sausage, casings removed
- 1 medium onion, chopped
- 1 garlic clove, minced
- 2 medium zucchini, chopped
- 1 large sweet red pepper, chopped
- 1 large sweet yellow pepper, chopped
- 1 can (28 oz.) diced tomatoes, drained
- ¼ tsp. salt
- ¼ tsp. pepper

1. Cook the pasta according to package directions; drain.
2. Meanwhile, in large skillet, cook sausage and onion over medium-high heat until sausage is no longer pink, 5-7 minutes. Add the garlic and cook 1 minute longer. Add zucchini and peppers; cook until crisp-tender, 3-5 minutes. Add the tomatoes, salt and pepper. Cook and stir until vegetables are tender and begin to release their juices, 5-7 minutes. Serve with pasta.
1⅓ cups: 251 cal., 6g fat (1g sat. fat), 28mg chol., 417mg sod., 35g carb. (4g sugars, 6g fiber), 16g pro. **Diabetic exchanges:** 2 vegetable, 2 lean meat, 1½ starch.

KIELBASA
CABBAGE SKILLET

Spicy kielbasa sausage and plentiful cabbage and potatoes give this dish a pleasing Old World flair. My husband never liked cabbage before I made this, but now he does!
—Romaine Wetzel, Ronks, PA

- -

Prep: 10 min. • **Cook:** 1¼ hours
Makes: 4 servings

- ½ lb. smoked kielbasa or smoked Polish sausage, cut into ½-in. slices
- 2 Tbsp. butter, divided
- ½ large head cabbage (2 lbs.), coarsely chopped
- 1 medium onion, chopped
- 2 cans (8 oz. each) tomato sauce
- ¼ cup sugar
- 1 Tbsp. paprika
- 2 large potatoes, peeled and cubed

1. In a large enameled cast iron or other ovenproof skillet, brown the sausage in 1 Tbsp. butter; remove and set aside. In the same pan, saute cabbage and onions in remaining butter until onions are tender.
2. In a small bowl, combine the tomato sauce, sugar and paprika; pour over cabbage mixture. Bring to a boil. Reduce heat; cover and simmer for 20 minutes. Add potatoes and reserved sausage. Cover and simmer for 30 minutes or until potatoes are tender.
1¾ cups: 489 cal., 23g fat (9g sat. fat), 53mg chol., 978mg sod., 62g carb. (22g sugars, 10g fiber), 15g pro.

BARBECUE PORK & PENNE SKILLET

I'm the proud mother of wonderful and active children. Simple, delicious and quick meals like this are perfect for us to enjoy together after errands, school activities and soccer practice are over.
—*Judy Armstrong, Prairieville, LA*

Takes: 25 min. • **Makes:** 8 servings

- 1 pkg. (16 oz.) penne pasta
- 1 cup chopped sweet red pepper
- ¾ cup chopped onion
- 1 Tbsp. butter
- 1 Tbsp. olive oil
- 3 garlic cloves, minced
- 1 carton (16 oz.) refrigerated fully cooked barbecued shredded pork
- 1 can (14½ oz.) diced tomatoes with mild green chiles, undrained
- ½ cup beef broth
- 1 tsp. ground cumin
- 1 tsp. pepper
- ¼ tsp. salt
- 1¼ cups shredded cheddar cheese
- ¼ cup chopped green onions

1. Cook the pasta according to package directions. Meanwhile, in a large skillet, saute red pepper and onion in butter and oil until tender. Add garlic; saute 1 minute longer. Stir in the pork, tomatoes, broth, cumin, pepper and salt; heat through.
2. Drain pasta. Add pasta and cheese to pork mixture; stir until blended. Sprinkle with the green onions.
Freeze option: Freeze cooled pasta mixture in freezer containers. To use, partially thaw in refrigerator overnight. Place in a shallow microwave-safe dish. Cover and microwave on high until heated through.
1¼ cups: 428 cal., 11g fat (6g sat. fat), 40mg chol., 903mg sod., 61g carb. (16g sugars, 4g fiber), 20g pro.

CLASSIC RED BEANS & RICE

After 25 years in a place where Cajun cooking is common, we've come to rely on this staple menu item. If you've never tried red beans and rice before, I'm sure you'll like this recipe.
—*Jackie Turnage, New Iberia, LA*

Prep: 10 min. • **Cook:** 2¼ hours + standing
Makes: 8 servings

- 1 lb. dried kidney beans
- 8 cups water
- 1 ham hock
- 2 bay leaves
- 1 tsp. onion powder
- 1 lb. ground beef
- 1 large onion, chopped
- 1 tsp. salt
- ½ tsp. pepper
- 1 garlic clove, minced
   Hot cooked rice
   Chopped fresh parsley, optional

1. Sort beans and rinse with cold water. Place beans in a Dutch oven; add water to cover by 2 in. Bring to a boil; boil for 2 minutes. Remove from the heat; cover and let stand until beans are softened, 1-4 hours.
2. Drain and rinse beans, discarding liquid. Return to Dutch oven. Add water, ham hock, bay leaves and onion powder. Bring to a boil. Reduce heat; cover and simmer for 1 hour.
3. In a large cast-iron or other heavy skillet, cook the beef, onion, salt and pepper over medium heat until meat is no longer pink. Add garlic; cook 1 minute longer. Drain. Add to bean mixture. Simmer, uncovered, for 1 hour. Discard bay leaves.
4. Remove ham hock; allow to cool. Remove meat from bone; discard bone. Cut meat into bite-sized pieces and return to broth. Heat through. Serve with rice and, if desired, top with chopped fresh parsley.
1 serving: 309 cal., 7g fat (3g sat. fat), 35mg chol., 346mg sod., 37g carb. (4g sugars, 9g fiber), 25g pro.

> **TEST KITCHEN TIP**
> Smoked or cured ham hocks are usually available in your grocer's meat department. If you can't find them, ask your butcher for leftover ham bones.

ASPARAGUS HAM DINNER

QUICK PASTA DINNER

🕐
ASPARAGUS HAM DINNER

I've been making this light meal for my family for years now, and it's always well received. With asparagus, tomato, pasta and chunks of ham, this dish a tempting blend of tastes and textures.

—*Rhonda Zavodny, David City, NE*

- -

Takes: 25 min. • **Makes:** 6 servings

- 2 cups uncooked corkscrew or spiral pasta
- ¾ lb. fresh asparagus, cut into 1-in. pieces
- 1 medium sweet yellow pepper, julienned
- 1 Tbsp. olive oil
- 6 medium tomatoes, diced
- 6 oz. boneless fully cooked ham, cubed
- ¼ cup minced fresh parsley
- ½ tsp. salt
- ½ tsp. dried oregano
- ½ tsp. dried basil
- ⅛ to ¼ tsp. cayenne pepper
- ¼ cup shredded Parmesan cheese

Cook pasta according to package directions. Meanwhile, in a large cast-iron or other heavy skillet, saute asparagus and yellow pepper in oil until crisp-tender. Add the tomatoes and ham; heat through. Drain pasta; add to mixture. Stir in parsley and seasonings. Sprinkle with cheese.

1⅓ cups: 204 cal., 5g fat (1g sat. fat), 17mg chol., 561mg sod., 29g carb. (5g sugars, 3g fiber), 12g pro. **Diabetic exchanges:** 1½ starch, 1 lean meat, 1 vegetable, ½ fat.

TEQUILA LIME SHRIMP
ZOODLES, PAGE 90

CAST IRON
FISH, SEAFOOD
& MEATLESS

Whether caught from a stream or picked up at the grocery store,
fish and other freshwater favorites are perfect for cast-iron
cooking. Going meatless? Simply turn to this chapter for
those delicious dinners as well.

GREEK TILAPIA

While on a trip through the Greek islands, my husband and I had a dish that we loved. I tried to duplicate it by combining several different recipes and came up with this.
—*Sally Burrell, Idaho Falls, ID*

- -

Prep: 30 min. • **Bake:** 10 min.
Makes: 4 servings

4	tilapia fillets (4 oz. each)
4	tsp. butter
1	large egg
¾	cup crumbled tomato and basil feta cheese
¼	cup fat-free milk
¼	tsp. cayenne pepper
1	large tomato, seeded and chopped
¼	cup chopped ripe olives
¼	cup pine nuts, toasted
1	Tbsp. minced fresh parsley
1	Tbsp. lemon juice
⅛	tsp. pepper

1. In a large cast-iron or other ovenproof skillet, brown fish in butter.
2. In a small bowl, combine the egg, cheese, milk and cayenne; spoon over fish. Sprinkle with tomato, olives and pine nuts. Bake, uncovered, at 425° until fish just begins to flake easily with a fork, 10-15 minutes.
3. In a small bowl, combine the parsley, lemon juice and pepper; drizzle over fish.
1 fillet: 279 cal., 16g fat (6g sat. fat), 123mg chol., 362mg sod., 5g carb. (2g sugars, 2g fiber), 29g pro.

"Unlike anything I've made before, but my hubby really liked it. I made some red potatoes with olive oil and Mediterranean seasoning as a side."
EZRACC, TASTEOFHOME.COM

CHEDDAR-BUTTERNUT SQUASH CLAFOUTIS

CHEDDAR-BUTTERNUT SQUASH CLAFOUTIS

I came up with this savory version of the classic French dessert clafoutis and shared it for dinner with a salad. My friends loved it, but in the end I could have eaten the whole pan myself while dreaming of being in Paris with every scrumptious bite.
—*Joseph Sciascia, San Mateo, CA*

- -

Prep: 20 min. • **Cook:** 50 min. + standing
Makes: 6 servings

3	cups cubed peeled butternut squash
2	tsp. olive oil
1	tsp. minced fresh rosemary or ½ tsp. dried rosemary, crushed
1	tsp. minced fresh thyme or ½ tsp. dried thyme
½	tsp. kosher salt
¼	tsp. coarsely ground pepper
4	large eggs
1½	cups 2% milk
½	cup all-purpose flour
¼	tsp. cayenne pepper
2	cups shredded sharp white cheddar cheese
¼	cup grated Parmesan and Romano cheese blend
1	Tbsp. butter
1	Tbsp. minced fresh chives

1. Preheat oven to 400°. Place butternut squash in a 12-in. cast-iron skillet. Drizzle with oil. Sprinkle with rosemary, thyme, salt and pepper; toss to coat. Roast until just tender, 15-20 minutes. Remove from pan and keep warm.
2. In a large bowl, whisk eggs, milk, flour and cayenne; stir in cheeses. Place butter in same skillet; place skillet in oven until the butter is melted, 1-2 minutes. Carefully tilt pan to coat bottom and sides with butter. Pour the egg mixture into skillet; top with roasted squash.
3. Bake until puffed and edges are browned, 30-35 minutes. Let stand 15 minutes before cutting. Sprinkle with chives and additional Parmesan and Romano cheese blend.
1 piece: 357 cal., 22g fat (11g sat. fat), 176mg chol., 586mg sod., 22g carb. (5g sugars, 2g fiber), 19g pro.

GREEK TILAPIA

CAJUN SHRIMP SKILLET

There's plenty of delicious sauce with these shrimp, so I always serve bread on the side to soak it all up. Make it your own by using your favorite amber beer or flavorful broth.
—Mark Oppe, North Pole, AK

Takes: 25 min. • **Makes:** 4 servings

- 3 Tbsp. butter
- 2 garlic cloves, minced
- ½ cup amber beer or beef broth
- 1 tsp. Worcestershire sauce
- 1 tsp. pepper
- ½ tsp. salt
- ½ tsp. dried thyme
- ½ tsp. dried rosemary, crushed
- ½ tsp. crushed red pepper flakes
- ¼ tsp. cayenne pepper
- ⅛ tsp. dried oregano
- 1 lb. uncooked large shrimp, peeled and deveined
  Hot cooked grits, optional

In a large cast-iron or other heavy skillet, heat butter over medium-high heat. Add garlic; cook and stir 1 minute. Stir in beer, Worcestershire sauce and seasonings; bring to a boil. Add shrimp; cook until shrimp turn pink, 3-4 minutes, stirring occasionally. If desired, serve over grits.

½ cup: 186 cal., 10g fat (6g sat. fat), 160mg chol., 505mg sod., 3g carb. (1g sugars, 0 fiber), 19g pro. **Diabetic exchanges:** 3 lean meat, 2 fat.

BLACKENED CATFISH WITH MANGO AVOCADO SALSA

A delightful, tasty rub makes this quick recipe fantastic. While the fish is sitting to allow the flavors to blend, you can easily assemble the salsa. My family thinks it's just marvelous.
—Laura Fisher, Westfield, MA

Prep: 20 min. + chilling • **Cook:** 10 min.
Makes: 4 servings (2 cups salsa)

- 2 tsp. dried oregano
- 2 tsp. ground cumin
- 2 tsp. paprika
- 2¼ tsp. pepper, divided
- ¾ tsp. salt, divided
- 4 catfish fillets (6 oz. each)
- 1 medium mango, peeled and cubed
- 1 medium ripe avocado, peeled and cubed
- ⅓ cup finely chopped red onion
- 2 Tbsp. minced fresh cilantro
- 2 Tbsp. lime juice
- 2 tsp. olive oil

1. Combine the oregano, cumin, paprika, 2 tsp. pepper and ½ tsp. salt; rub over fillets. Refrigerate for at least 30 minutes.
2. Meanwhile, in a small bowl, combine the mango, avocado, red onion, cilantro, lime juice and remaining salt and pepper. Chill until serving.
3. In a large cast-iron skillet, cook fillets in oil over medium heat until fish flakes easily with a fork, 5-7 minutes on each side. Serve with the salsa.

1 fillet with ½ cup salsa: 376 cal., 22g fat (4g sat. fat), 80mg chol., 541mg sod., 17g carb. (9g sugars, 6g fiber), 28g pro. **Diabetic exchanges:** 5 lean meat, 1 starch, ½ fat.

CAJUN SHRIMP SKILLET

VEGGIE-CASHEW
STIR-FRY

HOMEY MAC & CHEESE

My grandson Zachary has been to Iraq and Afghanistan with both the Marines and Navy, and I'm proud to say that I've made this for him every time he returns home.
—*Alice Beardsell, Osprey, FL*

Prep: 20 min. • **Bake:** 25 min.
Makes: 8 servings

- 2½ cups uncooked elbow macaroni
- ¼ cup butter, cubed
- ¼ cup all-purpose flour
- ½ tsp. salt
- ¼ tsp. pepper
- 3 cups 2% milk
- 5 cups shredded sharp cheddar cheese, divided
- 2 Tbsp. Worcestershire sauce
- ½ tsp. paprika

1. Preheat oven to 350°. Cook the macaroni according to package directions for al dente.
2. Meanwhile, in a large saucepan, heat the butter over medium heat. Stir in flour, salt and pepper until smooth; gradually whisk in milk. Bring to a boil, stirring constantly; cook and stir until thickened, 2-3 minutes.
3. Reduce heat. Stir in 3 cups cheese and Worcestershire sauce until cheese is melted.
4. Drain macaroni; stir into sauce. Carefully transfer to a greased 10-in. cast-iron or ovenproof skillet. Bake, uncovered, for 20 minutes. Top with remaining cheese; sprinkle with paprika. Bake until bubbly and cheese is melted, 5-10 minutes.

1 cup: 447 cal., 28g fat (20g sat. fat), 97mg chol., 701mg sod., 28g carb. (6g sugars, 1g fiber), 22g pro.

VEGGIE-CASHEW STIR-FRY

Getting my meat-loving husband and two sons, ages 5 and 7, to eat more veggies has always been a struggle until I whipped up this stir-fry one night. I was shocked when they cleaned their plates and asked for seconds.
—*Abbey Hoffman, Ashland, OH*

Prep: 20 min. • **Cook:** 15 min.
Makes: 4 servings

- ¼ cup reduced-sodium soy sauce
- ¼ cup water
- 2 Tbsp. brown sugar
- 2 Tbsp. lemon juice
- 2 Tbsp. olive oil
- 1 garlic clove, minced
- 2 cups sliced fresh mushrooms
- 1 cup coarsely chopped fresh baby carrots
- 1 small zucchini, cut into ¼-in. slices
- 1 small sweet red pepper, coarsely chopped
- 1 small green pepper, coarsely chopped
- 4 green onions, sliced
- 2 cups cooked brown rice
- 1 can (8 oz.) sliced water chestnuts, drained
- ½ cup honey-roasted cashews

1. In a small bowl, mix the soy sauce, water, brown sugar and lemon juice until smooth; set aside.
2. In a large cast-iron or other skillet, heat oil over medium-high heat. Stir-fry garlic for 1 minute. Add vegetables; cook until vegetables are crisp-tender, 6-8 minutes.
3. Stir soy sauce mixture and add to the pan. Bring to a boil. Add rice and water chestnuts; heat through. Top with cashews.

1½ cups: 385 cal., 16g fat (3g sat. fat), 0 chol., 671mg sod., 56g carb. (15g sugars, 6g fiber), 9g pro.

QUICK MOROCCAN SHRIMP SKILLET

When my niece was attending West Point, she was sent to Morocco for five months. I threw her a going-away party with Moroccan decorations, costumes and cuisine, including this saucy shrimp dish. Whenever I make it now, I think of her and I smile.
—*Barbara Lento, Houston, PA*

- -

Takes: 25 min. • **Makes:** 4 servings

- 1   Tbsp. canola oil
- 1   small onion, chopped
- ¼   cup pine nuts
- 1   lb. uncooked shrimp (16-20 per lb.), peeled and deveined
- 1   cup uncooked pearl (Israeli) couscous
- 2   Tbsp. lemon juice
- 3   tsp. Moroccan seasoning (ras el hanout)
- 1   tsp. garlic salt
- 2   cups hot water
     Minced fresh parsley, optional

1. In a large skillet, heat oil over medium-high heat; saute onion and pine nuts until onion is tender, 2-3 minutes. Stir in all remaining ingredients except parsley; bring just to a boil. Reduce heat; simmer, covered, until shrimp turn pink, 4-6 minutes.
2. Remove from heat; let stand 5 minutes. If desired, top with parsley.
1 cup: 335 cal., 11g fat (1g sat. fat), 138mg chol., 626mg sod., 34g carb. (1g sugars, 1g fiber), 24g pro.
Note: This recipe was tested with McCormick Gourmet Moroccan Seasoning (ras el hanout).

TEST KITCHEN TIP
Letting the mixture stand before serving helps the pasta absorb more of the wonderfully savory liquid. Even after sitting, it will still be a saucy dish, so serve it in a shallow bowl.

TEQUILA LIME SHRIMP ZOODLES

This tangy shrimp is a smart way to cut carbs without sacrificing flavor. If you don't have a spiralizer, use thinly julienned zucchini to get a similar effect.
—*Brigette Schroeder, Yorkville, IL*

- -

Takes: 30 min. • **Makes:** 4 servings

- 3   Tbsp. butter, divided
- 1   shallot, minced
- 2   garlic cloves, minced
- ¼   cup tequila
- 1½ tsp. grated lime zest
- 2   Tbsp. lime juice
- 1   Tbsp. olive oil
- 1   lb. uncooked shrimp (31-40 per lb.), peeled and deveined
- 2   medium zucchini, spiralized (about 6 cups)
- ½   tsp. salt
- ¼   tsp. pepper
- ¼   cup minced fresh parsley
     Additional grated lime zest

1. In a large cast-iron or other heavy skillet, heat 2 Tbsp. butter over medium heat. Add shallot and garlic; cook 1-2 minutes. Remove from heat; stir in tequila, lime zest and lime juice. Cook over medium heat until liquid is almost evaporated, 2-3 minutes.
2. Add olive oil and remaining butter; stir in shrimp and zucchini. Sprinkle with salt and pepper. Cook and stir 4-5 minutes or until shrimp begin to turn pink and zucchini is crisp-tender. Sprinkle with parsley and additional lime zest.
1¼ cups: 246 cal., 14g fat (6g sat. fat), 161mg chol., 510mg sod., 7g carb. (3g sugars, 1g fiber), 20g pro. **Diabetic exchanges:** 3 lean meat, 3 fat, 1 vegetable.

TOFU CHOW MEIN

TOFU CHOW MEIN

This is an ideal recipe for a tofu beginner, as it's an easy, approachable way to use it. If you have time, one way to prepare it is to cut the tofu block in half and wrap well in a terry kitchen towel. Let it sit in the fridge for at least an hour to absorb excess water. For a complete meal, serve this dish with a hot-and-sour soup and egg rolls.
—*Autumn SinClaire, Gold Beach, OR*

Prep: 15 min. + standing • **Cook:** 15 min.
Makes: 4 servings

- 8   oz. uncooked whole wheat angel hair pasta
- 3   Tbsp. sesame oil, divided
- 1   pkg. (16 oz.) extra-firm tofu
- 2   cups sliced fresh mushrooms
- 1   medium sweet red pepper, julienned
- ¼   cup reduced-sodium soy sauce
- 3   green onions, thinly sliced

1. Cook the pasta according to package directions. Drain; rinse with cold water and drain again. Toss with 1 Tbsp. oil; spread onto a baking sheet and let stand about 1 hour.
2. Meanwhile, cut tofu into ½-in. cubes and blot dry. Wrap in a clean kitchen towel; place on a plate and refrigerate until ready to cook.
3. In a large skillet, heat 1 Tbsp. oil over medium heat. Add pasta, spreading evenly; cook until bottom is lightly browned, about 5 minutes. Remove from pan.
4. In same skillet, heat remaining oil over medium-high heat; stir-fry mushrooms, pepper and tofu until mushrooms are tender, 3-4 minutes. Add pasta and soy sauce; toss and heat through. Sprinkle with green onions.
1½ cups: 417 cal., 17g fat (2g sat. fat), 0 chol., 588mg sod., 48g carb. (3g sugars, 8g fiber), 21g pro. **Diabetic exchanges:** 3 fat, 2½ starch, 2 lean meat, 1 vegetable.

BLEND OF THE BAYOU

BLEND OF THE BAYOU

My sister-in-law shared this recipe with me when I first moved to Louisiana. It's been handed down in my husband's family for generations. It's quick to prepare, nutritious and beautiful. I've passed it on to my children, too. It's rich, filling and sensational!
—*Ruby Williams, Bogalusa, LA*

Prep: 20 min. • **Bake:** 25 min.
Makes: 8 servings

- 1 pkg. (8 oz.) cream cheese, cubed
- 4 Tbsp. butter, divided
- 1 large onion, chopped
- 2 celery ribs, chopped
- 1 large green pepper, chopped
- 1 lb. cooked medium shrimp, peeled and deveined
- 2 cans (6 oz. each) crabmeat, drained, flaked and cartilage removed
- 1 can (10¾ oz.) condensed cream of mushroom soup, undiluted
- ¾ cup cooked rice
- 1 jar (4½ oz.) sliced mushrooms, drained
- 1 tsp. garlic salt
- ¾ tsp. hot pepper sauce
- ½ tsp. cayenne pepper
- ¾ cup shredded cheddar cheese
- ½ cup crushed butter-flavored crackers (about 12 crackers)

1. Preheat oven to 350°. In a saucepan, cook and stir cream cheese and 2 Tbsp. butter over low heat until melted and smooth.
2. In a large cast-iron or other ovenproof skillet, saute onion, celery and green pepper in remaining butter until tender. Stir in shrimp, crab, soup, rice, mushrooms, garlic salt, pepper sauce, cayenne and cream cheese mixture.
3. Combine cheddar cheese and cracker crumbs; sprinkle over top. Bake, uncovered, until bubbly, 25-30 minutes.

1 cup: 366 cal., 23g fat (13g sat. fat), 164mg chol., 981mg sod., 17g carb. (3g sugars, 2g fiber), 23g pro.

SAGE-RUBBED SALMON

SAGE-RUBBED SALMON

If you've always thought of sage with turkey, try it with salmon for a little taste of heaven. We serve this with rice, salad and sauteed green beans.
—*Nicole Raskopf, Beacon, NY*

Takes: 20 min. • **Makes:** 6 servings

- 2 Tbsp. minced fresh sage
- 1 tsp. garlic powder
- 1 tsp. kosher salt
- 1 tsp. freshly ground pepper
- 1 skin-on salmon fillet (1½ lbs.)
- 2 Tbsp. olive oil

1. Preheat the oven to 375°. Mix first the 4 ingredients; rub onto flesh side of salmon. Cut into 6 portions.
2. In a large cast-iron skillet, heat oil over medium heat. Add salmon, skin side down; cook 5 minutes. Transfer skillet to oven; bake just until fish flakes easily with a fork, about 10 minutes.

3 oz. cooked fish: 220 cal., 15g fat (3g sat. fat), 57mg chol., 377mg sod., 1g carb. (0 sugars, 0 fiber), 19g pro. **Diabetic exchanges:** 3 lean meat.

"It was perfect. I really liked the slight crust the oven put on the rub. I will definitely make again."
7833LOUIS, TASTEOFHOME.COM

SWEET POTATO & BEAN QUESADILLAS

This recipe is special to me because it's healthy, easy, fast and delicious!
—Brittany Hubbard, St. Paul, MN

Takes: 30 min. • Makes: 4 servings

2 medium sweet potatoes
4 whole wheat tortillas (8 in.)
¾ cup canned black beans, rinsed and drained
½ cup shredded pepper jack cheese
¾ cup salsa

1. Scrub sweet potatoes; pierce several times with a fork. Place on a microwave-safe plate. Microwave, uncovered, on high, turning once, until very tender, 7-9 minutes.
2. When cool enough to handle, cut each potato lengthwise in half. Scoop out pulp. Spread onto half of each tortilla; top with beans and cheese. Fold other half of tortilla over filling.
3. Heat a cast-iron skillet or griddle over medium heat. Cook quesadillas until golden brown and cheese is melted, 2-3 minutes on each side. Serve with salsa.

1 quesadilla with 3 Tbsp. salsa: 306 cal., 8g fat (3g sat. fat), 15mg chol., 531mg sod., 46g carb. (9g sugars, 6g fiber), 11g pro.

SPICY SALMON PATTIES

SPICY SALMON PATTIES

Made with canned salmon, these patties are good hot or cold. I usually serve them on buns with slices of ripe tomato, sweet red onion, and red and green bell pepper.
—Barbara Coston, Little Rock, AR

Takes: 30 min. • Makes: 4 servings

2 slices whole wheat bread
12 miniature pretzels
2 tsp. Italian seasoning
2 tsp. salt-free spicy seasoning blend
½ tsp. pepper
2 large eggs, lightly beaten
1 can (14¾ oz.) salmon, drained, bones and skin removed
½ cup finely chopped onion
⅓ cup finely chopped green pepper
1 Tbsp. finely chopped jalapeno pepper
2 garlic cloves, minced
2 Tbsp. olive oil

1. Place the first 5 ingredients in a blender or food processor; cover and process until mixture resembles fine crumbs.
2. In a bowl, combine the eggs, salmon, onion, green pepper, jalapeno, garlic and ½ cup crumb mixture. Shape into eight ½-in.-thick patties. Coat with remaining crumb mixture.
3. In a large nonstick skillet over medium heat, cook patties in oil until golden brown, 4-5 minutes on each side.

2 patties: 339 cal., 18g fat (3g sat. fat), 176mg chol., 607mg sod., 13g carb. (2g sugars, 2g fiber), 30g pro. **Diabetic exchanges:** 4 lean meat, 2 fat, 1 starch.

SPICY VEGGIE PASTA BAKE

My dad cooked with cast-iron skillets, so I always remember his amazing culinary skills when I reach for my skillet. One of the ways I keep the tradition going is with this pasta.
—Sonya Goergen, Moorhead, MN

Takes: 30 min. • Makes: 6 servings

- 3 cups uncooked spiral pasta
- 1 medium yellow summer squash
- 1 small zucchini
- 1 medium sweet red pepper
- 1 medium green pepper
- 1 Tbsp. olive oil
- 1 small red onion, halved and sliced
- 1 cup sliced fresh mushrooms
- ½ tsp. salt
- ¼ tsp. pepper
- ¼ tsp. crushed red pepper flakes
- 1 jar (24 oz.) spicy marinara sauce
- 8 oz. fresh mozzarella cheese pearls
  Optional: Grated Parmesan cheese and julienned fresh basil

1. Preheat oven to 375°. Cook the pasta according to the package directions for al dente; drain.
2. Cut the squashes and peppers into ¼-in. julienne strips. In a 12-in. cast-iron or other ovenproof skillet, heat oil over medium-high heat. Add onion, mushrooms and julienned vegetables; cook and stir until crisp-tender, 5-7 minutes. Stir in seasonings. Add marinara sauce and pasta; toss to combine. Top with cheese pearls.
3. Transfer to oven; bake, uncovered, until cheese is melted, 10-15 minutes. If desired, sprinkle with Parmesan cheese and basil before serving.
1⅓ cups: 420 cal., 13g fat (6g sat. fat), 32mg chol., 734mg sod., 57g carb. (12g sugars, 5g fiber), 17g pro.

BLACKENED HALIBUT

Serve these spicy fillets with garlic mashed potatoes, hot crusty bread and a crisp salad to lure in your crew. This is what my family eats when we want to celebrate.
—Brenda Williams, Santa Maria, CA

Takes: 25 min. • Makes: 4 servings

- 2 Tbsp. garlic powder
- 1 Tbsp. salt
- 1 Tbsp. onion powder
- 1 Tbsp. dried oregano
- 1 Tbsp. dried thyme
- 1 Tbsp. cayenne pepper
- 1 Tbsp. pepper
- 2½ tsp. paprika
- 4 halibut fillets (4 oz. each)
- 2 Tbsp. butter

1. In a large shallow dish, combine the first 8 ingredients. Add fillets, 2 at a time, and turn to coat.
2. In a large cast-iron skillet, cook fillets in butter over medium heat until fish flakes easily with a fork, 3-4 minutes on each side.
1 fillet: 189 cal., 8g fat (4g sat. fat), 51mg chol., 758mg sod., 3g carb. (1g sugars, 1g fiber), 24g pro. **Diabetic exchanges:** 3 lean meat, 1 fat.

SPICY VEGGIE PASTA BAKE

LEMON-PEPPER TILAPIA WITH MUSHROOMS

My husband and I are trying to add more fish and healthy entrees to our diet, and this dish makes it easy to do just that. Best of all, it comes together in just under 30 minutes, so it's great for hectic weeknights.
—*Donna McDonald, Lake Elsinore, CA*

Takes: 25 min. • **Makes:** 4 servings

- 2 Tbsp. butter
- ½ lb. sliced fresh mushrooms
- ¾ tsp. lemon-pepper seasoning, divided
- 3 garlic cloves, minced
- 4 tilapia fillets (6 oz. each)
- ¼ tsp. paprika
- ⅛ tsp. cayenne pepper
- 1 medium tomato, chopped
- 3 green onions, thinly sliced

1. In a 12-in. skillet, heat butter over medium heat. Add mushrooms and ¼ tsp. lemon pepper; cook and stir 3-5 minutes or until tender. Add garlic; cook 30 seconds longer.
2. Place fillets over mushrooms; sprinkle with paprika, cayenne and remaining lemon pepper. Cook, covered, 5-7 minutes or until fish just begins to flake easily with a fork. Top with tomato and green onions.
1 fillet: 216 cal., 8g fat (4g sat. fat), 98mg chol., 173mg sod., 5g carb. (2g sugars, 1g fiber), 34g pro. **Diabetic exchanges:** 4 lean meat, 1½ fat.

QUICK AND COLORFUL

LEMON-PEPPER TILAPIA WITH MUSHROOMS

GORGONZOLA SHRIMP PASTA

This creamy pasta dish is so easy. It's a speedy entree when time is tight but it feels special enough for company.
—*Robin Haas, Hyde Park, MA*

Takes: 30 min. • **Makes:** 6 servings

- 12 oz. uncooked penne pasta
- 2 Tbsp. olive oil
- 1 lb. uncooked shrimp (31-40 per lb.), peeled and deveined
- 3 garlic cloves, minced
- ½ cup dried cranberries
- ½ cup dry white wine or reduced-sodium chicken broth
- 6 oz. fresh baby spinach (about 3 cups)
- 4 oz. reduced-fat cream cheese, cubed
- ½ cup crumbled Gorgonzola cheese
- 3 Tbsp. minced fresh parsley
- ¼ tsp. salt
- ⅓ cup chopped walnuts

1. Cook the penne according to package directions for al dente. Meanwhile, in a large cast-iron skillet or Dutch oven, heat oil over medium heat. Add shrimp and garlic; cook until shrimp are pink, 5-10 minutes. Remove from pan and keep warm.
2. Stir cranberries and wine into same pan. Bring to a boil; cook until liquid is almost evaporated, about 5 minutes.
3. Drain penne, reserving 1 cup of pasta water; add penne to pan. Stir in spinach, cream cheese, Gorgonzola cheese, parsley, salt and reserved shrimp. Cook and stir until mixture is heated through and cheeses are melted, about 5 minutes, adding enough reserved pasta water to reach desired consistency. Top with chopped walnuts.
2 cups: 486 cal., 18g fat (6g sat. fat), 114mg chol., 422mg sod., 57g carb. (13g sugars, 4g fiber), 26g pro.

MUSHROOM PEAR MELTS

I really like mushrooms with cheese. Add some pears, broil away, and you have a scrumptious meatless, open-faced sandwich. Serve it with a salad and fruity tea.
—*Marla Hyatt, St. Paul, MN*

Takes: 25 min. • **Makes:** 4 servings

- 2 Tbsp. butter
- 4 cups sliced fresh shiitake or baby portobello mushrooms (about 10 oz.)
- ½ tsp. salt
- ¼ tsp. pepper
- 8 slices whole wheat bread, toasted
- 2 large ripe Bosc pears, thinly sliced
- 8 slices provolone cheese

1. Preheat broiler. In a large cast-iron or other heavy skillet, heat the butter over medium-high heat. Add mushrooms; cook and stir until tender, 5-7 minutes. Stir in salt and pepper.
2. Place toast slices on a rack of a broiler pan. Top with mushrooms; layer with pears and cheese. Broil 3-4 in. from heat until cheese is lightly browned, 2-3 minutes.
2 open-faced sandwiches: 421 cal., 20g fat (11g sat. fat), 45mg chol., 883mg sod., 46g carb. (15g sugars, 9g fiber), 19g pro.

TEST KITCHEN TIP
Don't have any pears in the kitchen? Try these change-of-pace sammies with thinly sliced apples instead.

BERRY-APPLE-RHUBARB
PIE, P. 104

CAST IRON
CRISPS, COBBLERS &
OTHER SWEETS

What a treat—a homemade dessert from a cast-iron skillet!
Family and friends will come running when you set out
any of the heartwarming choices here.

NEW ORLEANS BEIGNETS

SHOOFLY CHOCOLATE PIE

If you like classic shoofly pie, you'll want to try the chocolate version. It's even better! Let a scoop of vanilla ice cream slowly melt on top of your warm-from-the-oven slice.
—*Gwen Brounce Widdowson, Fleetwood, PA*

Prep: 20 min. • **Bake:** 45 min. + cooling
Makes: 8 servings

    Pastry for single-crust pie (9 in.)
½ cup semisweet chocolate chips
1½ cups all-purpose flour
½ cup packed brown sugar
3 Tbsp. butter-flavored shortening
1 tsp. baking soda
1½ cups water
1 large egg, room temperature, lightly beaten
1 cup molasses

1. Roll out dough to fit a 9-in. deep-dish pie plate or cast-iron skillet. Trim to ½ in. beyond rim of plate; flute edges. Sprinkle chocolate chips into crust; set aside.
2. In a large bowl, combine flour and brown sugar; cut in shortening until crumbly. Set aside 1 cup for topping. Add the baking soda, water, egg and molasses to the remaining crumb mixture and mix well. Pour over chips. Sprinkle with reserved crumb mixture.
3. Bake at 350° until a knife inserted in the center comes out clean, 45-55 minutes. Let stand on a wire rack for 15 minutes before cutting. Serve warm.
1 piece: 526 cal., 20g fat (10g sat. fat), 53mg chol., 341mg sod., 83g carb. (49g sugars, 2g fiber), 6g pro.

TEST KITCHEN TIP

A staple in Pennsylvania Dutch cooking, shoofly pie has a cakelike filling with a strong molasses flavor. Shoofly pies are best served warm alongside a cup of hot coffee or a glass of cold milk.

NEW ORLEANS BEIGNETS

These sugar-coated French doughnuts are square instead of round and have no hole in the middle. They're a traditional part of breakfast in New Orleans.
—*Beth Dawson, Jackson, LA*

Prep: 25 min. + chilling • **Cook:** 5 min./batch
Makes: 4 dozen

1 pkg. (¼ oz.) active dry yeast
¼ cup warm water (110° to 115°)
1 cup evaporated milk
½ cup canola oil
¼ cup sugar
1 large egg, room temperature
4½ cups self-rising flour
    Oil for deep-fat frying
    Confectioners' sugar

1. In a large bowl, dissolve yeast in warm water. Add evaporated milk, oil, sugar, egg and 2 cups flour. Beat until smooth. Stir in enough remaining flour to form a soft dough (dough will be sticky). Do not knead. Cover and refrigerate overnight.
2. Punch dough down. Turn onto a floured surface; roll into a 16x12-in. rectangle. Cut into 2-in. squares.
3. In a deep cast-iron or electric skillet, heat 1 in. oil to 375°. Fry the squares, in batches, until golden brown on both sides. Drain on paper towels. While still warm, roll the beignets in confectioners' sugar.
1 beignet: 104 cal., 5g fat (1g sat. fat), 6mg chol., 142mg sod., 14g carb. (5g sugars, 0 fiber), 2g pro.

SHOOFLY
CHOCOLATE PIE

RUSTIC HONEY CAKE

When my boys were young, they couldn't have milk, but they could eat yogurt. This from-scratch favorite was a treat they were free to enjoy. Not overly sweet, it's a nice choice for breakfast, too.
—*Linda Leuer, Hamel, MN*

Prep: 15 min. • **Bake:** 30 min. + cooling
Makes: 12 servings

- ½ cup butter, softened
- 1 cup honey
- 2 large eggs, room temperature
- ½ cup plain yogurt
- 1 tsp. vanilla extract
- 2 cups all-purpose flour
- 2 tsp. baking powder
- ½ tsp. salt
  Assorted fresh fruit and additional honey
  Chopped pistachios, optional

1. Preheat oven to 350°. Grease a 9-in. cast-iron skillet.
2. In a large bowl, beat butter and honey until blended. Add eggs, 1 at a time, beating well after each addition. Beat in yogurt and vanilla. In another bowl, whisk flour, baking powder and salt; add to the butter mixture. Transfer batter to prepared skillet.
3. Bake until a toothpick inserted in center comes out clean, 30-35 minutes. Cool cake completely in the pan on a wire rack. Serve with fruit, additional honey and, if desired, chopped pistachios.
Freeze option: Securely wrap the cooled cake in foil; freeze. To use, thaw at room temperature and top as directed.
1 piece: 248 cal., 9g fat (5g sat. fat), 53mg chol., 257mg sod., 40g carb. (24g sugars, 1g fiber), 4g pro.

CAST-IRON APPLE NUTMEG COFFEE CAKE

One morning I decided to stir my last bit of coffee into the ingredients for a coffee cake. I loved the result! It was super moist, had a pleasantly crumbly texture and tasted like I'd dunked it right into a cup of hot joe. For a little bit of crunch, add some chopped pecans to the apples.
—*Darla Andrews, Schertz, TX*

Prep: 25 min. • **Bake:** 20 min. + cooling
Makes: 8 servings

- 3 Tbsp. butter, cubed
- 2 cups chopped peeled Gala apple
- ½ cup packed brown sugar, divided
- ¼ cup brewed coffee
- ⅔ cup canola oil
- ½ cup sugar
- 1 large egg plus 1 large egg white, room temperature
- 2 tsp. vanilla extract
- 1½ cups all-purpose flour
- 2 tsp. ground cinnamon
- ½ tsp. salt
- ½ tsp. baking soda
- ¼ tsp. ground nutmeg

DRIZZLE
- ⅓ cup brewed coffee
- ¼ cup heavy whipping cream
- 1½ cups confectioners' sugar

1. Preheat oven to 375°. In a 10-in. cast-iron or other ovenproof skillet, melt the butter over low heat. Add apple and ¼ cup brown sugar. Cook and stir until crisp-tender, about 5 minutes. Stir in coffee; remove from heat.
2. In a large bowl, beat oil, sugar, egg, egg white, vanilla and remaining ¼ cup brown sugar until well blended. In another bowl, whisk flour, cinnamon, salt, baking soda and nutmeg; gradually beat into the oil mixture. Gently spread over the apple mixture.
3. Bake until a toothpick inserted in center comes out clean, 18-22 minutes. Cool on a wire rack 10 minutes.
4. Meanwhile, for drizzle, in a small saucepan, bring the coffee and heavy whipping cream to a boil; cook until the liquid is reduced to ¼ cup, 10-12 minutes. Remove from the heat; stir in confectioners' sugar. Let stand 10 minutes. Drizzle over cake.
1 piece: 532 cal., 27g fat (6g sat. fat), 43mg chol., 284mg sod., 71g carb. (51g sugars, 1g fiber), 4g pro.

CAST-IRON APPLE
NUTMEG COFFEE CAKE

CHOCOLATE PECAN
SKILLET COOKIE

GRILLED CRANBERRY PEAR CRUMBLE

My husband is always happy when I make dessert, and fruit crisps are often my go-to because they're quick and easy to prepare. I came up with this fall-flavored version that cooks in a skillet on the grill.
—*Ronna Farley, Rockville, MD*

- -

Takes: 30 min. • **Makes:** 6 servings

- 3   medium ripe pears, sliced
- ½   cup dried cranberries
- ¼   cup sugar
- 2   Tbsp. all-purpose flour
- ¼   tsp. ground cinnamon
- 1   Tbsp. butter

TOPPING

- 2   Tbsp. butter, melted
- ¼   tsp. ground cinnamon
- 1   cup granola without raisins

1. Toss pears and cranberries with sugar, flour and cinnamon. Place 1 Tbsp. butter in a 9-in. cast-iron skillet. Place on grill rack over medium heat until butter is melted. Stir in fruit; grill, covered, until pears are tender, 15-20 minutes, stirring occasionally.
2. For the topping, mix melted butter and cinnamon; toss with granola. Sprinkle over pears. Grill, covered, 5 minutes. Serve warm.
1 serving: 258 cal., 9g fat (4g sat. fat), 15mg chol., 54mg sod., 47g carb. (29g sugars, 7g fiber), 4g pro.

CHOCOLATE PECAN SKILLET COOKIE

Here's the ultimate shareable cookie! If you like, replace the chocolate chips with an equal amount of M&M's. Or get fancy—gently fold in 1½ cups fresh raspberries after mixing the chips and nuts into the dough.
—*James Schend, Pleasant Prairie, WI*

- -

Prep: 15 min. • **Bake:** 35 min.
Makes: 12 servings

- 1   cup butter
- 1   cup sugar
- 1   cup packed brown sugar
- 2   large eggs, room temperature
- 2   tsp. vanilla extract
- 3   cups all-purpose flour
- 1½ tsp. baking soda
- ½   tsp. kosher salt
- 1   cup 60% cacao bittersweet chocolate baking chips
- 1   cup chopped pecans, toasted
     Vanilla ice cream, optional

1. Preheat oven to 350°. In a 12-in. cast-iron skillet, heat butter in oven as it preheats. Meanwhile, in a large bowl, stir together sugar and brown sugar. When the butter is almost melted, remove skillet from oven and swirl butter until completely melted. Stir butter into sugar mixture; set skillet aside.
2. Beat eggs and vanilla into sugar mixture. In another bowl, whisk together flour, baking soda and salt; gradually beat into the sugar mixture. Stir in chocolate chips and nuts. Spread mixture into buttered skillet.
3. Bake until toothpick inserted in center comes out with moist crumbs and the top is golden brown, 35-40 minutes. Serve warm, with vanilla ice cream if desired.
1 serving: 528 cal., 27g fat (13g sat. fat), 72mg chol., 378mg sod., 69g carb. (43g sugars, 3g fiber), 6g pro.

BERRY-APPLE-RHUBARB PIE

I bake this every year for a get-together at my sister's house, where the recipe is known as Uncle Mike's pie. I use fresh berries, apples and rhubarb I grow myself.
—*Michael Powers, New Baltimore, VA*

- -

Prep: 30 min. + chilling
Bake: 65 min. + cooling • **Makes:** 8 servings

2⅔ cups all-purpose flour
1 tsp. salt
1 cup butter-flavored shortening
6 to 8 Tbsp. cold water
FILLING
2 cups thinly sliced peeled tart apples
1 Tbsp. lemon juice
1 tsp. vanilla extract
1 cup halved fresh strawberries
1 cup fresh blueberries
1 cup fresh raspberries
1 cup fresh blackberries
1 cup sliced fresh or frozen rhubarb
⅓ cup all-purpose flour
1 tsp. ground allspice
1 tsp. ground cinnamon
1½ cups plus 1 tsp. sugar, divided
2 Tbsp. butter
1 Tbsp. 2% milk

1. In a large bowl, combine flour and salt; cut in shortening until crumbly. Gradually add cold water, tossing with a fork until dough forms a ball. Divide dough in half so that 1 portion is slightly larger than the other; wrap and refrigerate until easy to handle, about 30 minutes.
2. Preheat oven to 400°. On a lightly floured surface, roll out the larger portion of dough to fit a 9-in. cast-iron skillet or deep-dish pie plate. Transfer pastry to skillet.
3. In a large bowl, toss apples with lemon juice and vanilla; add berries and rhubarb. Combine the flour, allspice, cinnamon and 1½ cups sugar; add to the apple mixture and toss gently to coat. Spoon into the crust; dot with butter.
4. Roll out remaining pastry; make a lattice crust. Trim, seal and flute the edges. Brush milk over the lattice top. Sprinkle with the remaining sugar.
5. Bake 15 minutes. Reduce heat to 350°; bake 50-60 minutes longer or until crust is golden brown and filling is bubbly. Cover edges with foil during the last 15 minutes to prevent overbrowning if necessary. Cool on a wire rack.
1 piece: 615 cal., 28g fat (8g sat. fat), 8mg chol., 318mg sod., 86g carb. (46g sugars, 5g fiber), 6g pro.

GINGER MANGO GRUNT

Tender dumplings in a chunky fruit sauce make a wonderfully down-home dessert. I like to top off my bowlful with a scoop of low-fat frozen yogurt.
—*Roxanne Chan, Albany, CA*

- -

Prep: 25 min. • **Cook:** 20 min.
Makes: 8 servings

½ cup all-purpose flour
3 Tbsp. yellow cornmeal
4½ tsp. sugar
1 tsp. baking powder
¼ tsp. ground ginger
⅛ tsp. salt
2 Tbsp. cold butter
3 Tbsp. egg substitute
¾ cup mango nectar, divided
1 jar (20 oz.) refrigerated mango slices, drained
½ cup reduced-sugar orange marmalade
1 Tbsp. lemon juice
½ cup golden raisins
¼ cup chopped crystallized ginger
¼ cup sliced almonds
   Low-fat frozen yogurt, optional

1. In a small bowl, combine the first 6 ingredients. Cut in butter until mixture resembles coarse crumbs. Combine egg substitute and ¼ cup nectar; stir into the flour mixture just until moistened.
2. Coarsely chop mango slices; combine with orange marmalade, lemon juice and remaining nectar.
3. Transfer to an 8-in. cast-iron or other ovenproof skillet; stir in raisins. Bring to a boil. Drop flour mixture in 8 mounds onto simmering mango mixture. Reduce heat; cover and simmer for 12-15 minutes or until a toothpick inserted in a dumpling comes out clean (do not lift the cover while simmering). Sprinkle with crystallized ginger and sliced almonds; if desired, serve with frozen yogurt.
1 serving: 232 cal., 5g fat (2g sat. fat), 8mg chol., 136mg sod., 47g carb. (31g sugars, 2g fiber), 3g pro.

CLASSIC SWEET POTATO PIE

CLASSIC SWEET POTATO PIE

With a pecan-filled crust and plenty of spice, this deep-dish favorite is ideal for fall and winter menus. Garnish with whipped cream and toasted nuts for the perfect finish.
—*Paul Azzone, Shoreham, NY*

- -

Prep: 25 min. • **Bake:** 45 min. + cooling
Makes: 8 servings

1⅔ cups pie crust mix
¼ cup finely chopped pecans
3 to 4 Tbsp. cold water
3 large eggs, room temperature
2 cans (15 oz. each) sweet potatoes, drained
1 can (14 oz.) sweetened condensed milk
1½ to 2 tsp. pumpkin pie spice
1 tsp. vanilla extract
½ tsp. salt
  Optional: Whipped cream and additional chopped pecans, toasted

1. In a small bowl, combine pie crust mix and pecans. Gradually add cold water, tossing with a fork until dough forms a ball. Roll out to fit a 9-in. cast-iron skillet or deep-dish pie plate. Transfer crust to skillet. Flute edges; set aside.

2. In a food processor, combine the eggs, sweet potatoes, milk, pumpkin pie spice, vanilla and salt; blend until smooth. Pour into the crust.

3. Bake at 425° for 15 minutes. Reduce heat to 350°; bake 30-35 minutes longer or until a knife inserted in center comes out clean. Cool on a wire rack. Garnish with whipped cream and toasted pecans if desired.

1 piece: 417 cal., 17g fat (6g sat. fat), 96mg chol., 436mg sod., 59g carb. (42g sugars, 3g fiber), 9g pro.

CHOCOLATE CHIP
DUTCH BABY

CHOCOLATE CHIP DUTCH BABY

A friend introduced me to the traditional Dutch baby, a large puffed pancake. I altered it a bit to create this chocolate chip version my family requests all the time. Just add butter and maple syrup, then enjoy!
—*Mary Thompson, LaCrosse, WI*

- -

Takes: 30 min. • **Makes:** 4 servings

- ¼ cup miniature semisweet chocolate chips
- ¼ cup packed brown sugar

DUTCH BABY
- ½ cup all-purpose flour
- 2 large eggs, room temperature
- ½ cup half-and-half cream
- ⅛ tsp. ground nutmeg
  Dash ground cinnamon
- 3 Tbsp. butter
  Optional: Maple syrup and additional butter

1. In a small bowl, combine chocolate chips and brown sugar; set aside. In a small bowl, beat the flour, eggs, cream, nutmeg and cinnamon until smooth.
2. Place butter in an 8-in. cast-iron skillet or 9-in. pie plate. Heat in a 425° oven until melted, about 4 minutes. Pour batter into hot skillet or pie plate. Sprinkle with the chocolate chip mixture. Bake until top edges are golden brown, 13-15 minutes. Serve immediately with syrup and butter if desired.
1 piece: 313 cal., 17g fat (10g sat. fat), 144mg chol., 140mg sod., 33g carb. (21g sugars, 1g fiber), 6g pro.

Apple Dutch Baby: Omit chips, brown sugar, syrup and additional butter. Mix and bake the Dutch baby as directed. Meanwhile, in a small saucepan, cook and stir 1 chopped peeled medium tart apple, ½ cup apple jelly and ⅛ tsp. ground cinnamon until jelly is melted. Top each serving with apple mixture.
Fruited Dutch Baby: Omit chips, brown sugar, syrup and additional butter. Mix and bake the Dutch baby as directed. Combine 2 sliced medium firm bananas and 1 cup sliced fresh strawberries. Top Dutch baby servings with the fruit and, if desired, whipped cream; sprinkle each serving with 1 Tbsp. toasted flaked coconut.

CREAMY APPLE CRUMB PIE

CREAMY APPLE CRUMB PIE

Inspired by a classic apple pie from a church cookbook, I came up with my own variation. I knew the recipe was a keeper when my mother-in-law asked for a copy.
—*Linda Pawelski, Milwaukee, WI*

- -

Prep: 20 min. • **Bake:** 50 min. + cooling
Makes: 8 servings

- Pastry for single-crust pie (9 in.)
- ⅓ cup sugar
- 3 Tbsp. cornstarch
- 1 tsp. ground cinnamon
- ¼ tsp. ground allspice
- 6 cups diced peeled tart apples (about 6 medium)
- 1 cup reduced-fat sour cream
- 1 tsp. vanilla extract

TOPPING
- ½ cup all-purpose flour
- ¼ cup packed brown sugar
- ½ tsp. ground cinnamon
- 2 Tbsp. cold butter

1. Line a 9-in. cast-iron skillet or deep-dish pie plate with crust; flute edges. In a large bowl, combine the sugar, cornstarch, cinnamon and allspice. Fold in the apples. Combine sour cream and vanilla; stir into apple mixture. Spoon into crust.
2. For topping, combine the flour, brown sugar and cinnamon in a bowl; cut in butter until mixture resembles coarse crumbs. Sprinkle over filling.
3. Bake at 400° for 25 minutes. Reduce heat to 350°; bake 25-30 minutes longer or until filling is bubbly and topping is golden. Cool on a wire rack. Refrigerate leftovers.
1 piece: 299 cal., 11g fat (6g sat. fat), 22mg chol., 126mg sod., 49g carb. (28g sugars, 2g fiber), 4g pro. **Diabetic exchanges:** 2 starch, 2 fat, 1 fruit.

MILK CAKE

Here's a simple but special recipe for a skillet dessert. After baking, the cake goes under the broiler for a yummy coconut topping.
—*Suzanne Coleman, Rabun Gap, GA*

- -

Prep: 20 min. • **Bake:** 30 min.
Makes: 8 servings

- ½ cup 2% milk
- ¾ cup all-purpose flour
- 1 tsp. baking powder
- ¼ tsp. salt
- 3 large eggs, room temperature
- 1 tsp. vanilla extract
- 1 cup sugar

TOPPING
- ⅓ cup packed brown sugar
- ½ cup chopped pecans
- 2 Tbsp. butter, softened
- 2 Tbsp. 2% milk
- 1 cup sweetened shredded coconut

1. Scald milk by bringing it almost to a boil; set aside to cool. Combine flour, baking powder and salt; set aside. In a bowl, beat eggs until thick and lemon-colored; stir in vanilla. Gradually add sugar, blending well. On low speed, alternately mix in the milk and dry ingredients. Pour batter into a greased 10-in. cast-iron skillet.
2. Bake at 350° for 25-30 minutes or until cake springs back when lightly touched. Remove cake and preheat broiler. Combine all topping ingredients; sprinkle over cake. Broil 5 in. from heat until topping bubbles and turns golden brown. Serve warm.
1 piece: 349 cal., 15g fat (7g sat. fat), 90mg chol., 220mg sod., 51g carb. (39g sugars, 2g fiber), 5g pro.

SKILLET STOUT BROWNIES

SKILLET STOUT BROWNIES

Splashed with a little stout beer, these distinctive brownies are so rich and fudgy. Serve each wedge with a big scoop of vanilla ice cream. Pure heaven!
—*Mandy Naglich, New York, NY*

- -

Prep: 30 min. • **Bake:** 25 min. + cooling
Makes: 12 servings

- 8 oz. semisweet chocolate, chopped
- 1 cup butter, cubed
- 1 cup milk stout beer
- 1 large egg, room temperature
- 2 large egg yolks, room temperature
- ¾ cup sugar
- ¼ cup packed brown sugar
- ¾ cup all-purpose flour
- ⅓ cup baking cocoa
- ½ tsp. salt
  Vanilla ice cream, optional

1. Preheat oven to 350°. Place chocolate in a large bowl. In a 10-in. cast-iron or other ovenproof skillet, combine butter and stout. Bring to a boil; reduce the heat. Simmer 10 minutes, stirring constantly. Pour over chocolate; stir with a whisk until smooth. Cool slightly. In another large bowl, beat egg, egg yolks and sugars until blended. Stir in chocolate mixture. In another bowl, mix flour, baking cocoa and salt; gradually add to chocolate mixture, mixing well.
2. Spread into the skillet. Bake until set, 25-30 minutes. Cool completely in skillet on a wire rack. If desired, serve with vanilla ice cream.
1 piece: 363 cal., 24g fat (14g sat. fat), 87mg chol., 229mg sod., 29g carb. (21g sugars, 1g fiber), 4g pro.

CARAMEL-PECAN CHEESECAKE PIE

Indulge! With easy-to-find ingredients and only 15 minutes of prep, you can surprise family and friends with a holiday-worthy pie any time of year.
—*Becky Ruff, McGregor, IA*

Prep: 15 min. • **Bake:** 35 min. + chilling
Makes: 8 servings

- 1 sheet refrigerated pie crust
- 1 pkg. (8 oz.) cream cheese, softened
- ½ cup sugar
- 4 large eggs, room temperature
- 1 tsp. vanilla extract
- 1¼ cups chopped pecans
- 1 jar (12¼ oz.) fat-free caramel ice cream topping
   Additional fat-free caramel ice cream topping, optional

1. Preheat oven to 375°. Line a 9-in. cast-iron skillet or deep-dish pie plate with crust. Trim and flute edges. In a small bowl, beat cream cheese, sugar, 1 egg and vanilla until smooth. Spread into crust; sprinkle with pecans.
2. In a small bowl, whisk remaining eggs; gradually whisk in caramel topping until blended. Pour slowly over pecans.
3. Bake 35-40 minutes or until pie is lightly browned (loosely cover edges with foil after 20 minutes if pie browns too quickly). Cool on a wire rack 1 hour. Refrigerate 4 hours or overnight before slicing. If desired, garnish with additional caramel topping.
1 piece: 502 cal., 33g fat (11g sat. fat), 142mg chol., 277mg sod., 45g carb. (26g sugars, 2g fiber), 8g pro.

CARAMEL-PECAN
CHEESECAKE PIE

BERRY BLISS COBBLER

A little bit sweet, a little bit tart and topped with golden sugar-kissed biscuits, this berry cobbler is a summertime delight.
—*Taste of Home Test Kitchen*

Prep: 10 min. + standing • **Bake:** 20 min.
Makes: 6 servings

- 3 cups fresh strawberries, halved
- 1½ cups fresh raspberries
- 1½ cups fresh blueberries
- ⅔ cup plus 1 Tbsp. sugar, divided
- 3 Tbsp. quick-cooking tapioca
- 1 cup all-purpose flour
- 1 Tbsp. sugar
- 2 tsp. baking powder
- ¼ tsp. salt
- ¼ cup cold butter, cubed
- 1 large egg, room temperature
- ¼ cup plus 2 Tbsp. 2% milk
   Coarse sugar

1. Preheat oven to 400°. Toss strawberries, raspberries and blueberries with ⅔ cup sugar and tapioca. Transfer to a greased 10-in. cast-iron or other ovenproof skillet; let stand 20 minutes.
2. Meanwhile, whisk flour, 1 Tbsp. sugar, baking powder and salt. Cut in cold butter until mixture resembles coarse crumbs. In another bowl, whisk together egg and milk; stir into the crumb mixture just until moistened. Drop by tablespoonfuls onto fruit. Sprinkle with coarse sugar.
3. Bake, uncovered, until the filling is bubbly and topping is golden brown, 20-25 minutes. Serve warm.
1 serving: 335 cal., 9g fat (5g sat. fat), 52mg chol., 298mg sod., 60g carb. (34g sugars, 5g fiber), 5g pro.

PEACH SUGAR COOKIE CRUMBLE

If you like peach crisp, you'll love it with a sugar cookie topping. The recipe calls for convenient canned peaches, too.
—*Teri Rasey, Cadillac, MI*

- -

Prep: 30 min. • **Bake:** 35 min. + cooling
Makes: 12 servings

  2 Tbsp. butter
  4 cans (15¼ oz. each) sliced peaches, drained
1¾ cups sugar, divided
  3 tsp. vanilla extract, divided
  1 tsp. crystallized ginger, finely chopped
  ½ tsp. ground cinnamon
  1 cup shortening
  ¼ cup packed brown sugar
  1 large egg, room temperature
  1 tsp. almond extract
2½ cups all-purpose flour
  1 Tbsp. cornstarch
  1 tsp. baking soda
  ½ tsp. baking powder
     Optional: Chopped pecans, coarse sugar and vanilla ice cream

1. Preheat oven to 350°. Melt butter in a 12-in. cast-iron or other ovenproof skillet over medium heat. Add peaches, ¾ cup sugar, 2 tsp. vanilla, ginger and cinnamon. Cook and stir until peaches soften and begin to break down, about 10 minutes. Remove from the heat.
2. In a large bowl, cream shortening, brown sugar and remaining 1 cup sugar until light and fluffy, 5-7 minutes. Beat in egg, almond extract and remaining 1 tsp. vanilla.
3. In another bowl, whisk flour, cornstarch, baking soda and baking powder; gradually beat into creamed mixture. Crumble dough over peach mixture. If desired, sprinkle with pecans and coarse sugar. Bake until a toothpick inserted in center comes out clean, 35-40 min. Cool on a wire rack. If desired, serve with vanilla ice cream.
1 serving: 480 cal., 19g fat (5g sat. fat), 21mg chol., 156mg sod., 73g carb. (52g sugars, 2g fiber), 3g pro.

PEACH SUGAR COOKIE CRUMBLE

CANDIED SWEET POTATO PIES

My grandmother's candied sweet potatoes and fried pies were the best. I combine both of those treats into one amazing dessert!
—*Angela Eshelman, Phoenix, AZ*

- -

Prep: 1 hour 25 min. + chilling
Cook: 10 min./batch • **Makes:** 12 pies

- 6 cups all-purpose flour
- 2 tsp. salt
- 2 cups shortening
- ⅔ cup water
- 2 large eggs, room temperature
- 2 Tbsp. white vinegar
- 1 large sweet potato, peeled and cut into 1-in. cubes
- ¾ cup sugar
- ¼ cup butter, cubed
- 1½ tsp. lemon juice
- ½ tsp. salt
- ¼ tsp. vanilla extract
  Oil for deep-fat frying
  Confectioners' sugar

1. In a large bowl, combine flour and salt; cut in shortening until mixture resembles coarse crumbs. Combine water, eggs and vinegar; gradually add to dry ingredients, tossing with a fork until a ball forms. Cover and chill until easy to handle, 1-1½ hours.
2. Meanwhile, place sweet potato in a small saucepan; cover with water. Bring to a boil. Reduce the heat; cover and cook just until tender, 10-15 minutes. Drain.
3. In a large skillet, combine sugar, butter and potatoes; cook and stir until syrup is golden brown, 15-20 minutes. Remove from heat and mash. Stir in lemon juice, salt and vanilla. Cool to room temperature.
4. Roll out the dough to ¼-in. thickness. Cut 12 circles with a floured 5½-in. round cookie cutter. Spoon 2 Tbsp. filling onto half of each circle. Moisten the edges with water; fold the crust over the filling and press edges with a fork to seal.
5. In a deep cast-iron or electric skillet, heat 1 in. of oil to 375°. Fry pies in batches until golden brown, about 5 minutes, turning once. Drain on paper towels. Dust with confectioners' sugar.
1 pie: 771 cal., 51g fat (12g sat. fat), 41mg chol., 538mg sod., 67g carb. (16g sugars, 3g fiber), 8g pro.

SKILLET CHOCOLATE DUMPLINGS

Rich and oh, so tempting, these dumplings in chocolate sauce simmer to perfection on the stovetop. My family often requests them for birthdays and other events.
—*Becky Magee, Chandler, AZ*

- -

Prep: 20 min. • **Cook:** 20 min.
Makes: 8 servings

- ¾ cup packed brown sugar
- ¼ cup baking cocoa
- 1 Tbsp. cornstarch
  Dash salt
- 2 cups water
- 2 Tbsp. butter

DUMPLINGS
- 1¼ cups all-purpose flour
- 2 tsp. baking powder
- ½ tsp. salt
- ½ cup sugar
- 2 Tbsp. baking cocoa
- 3 Tbsp. butter
- 1 large egg, lightly beaten
- ⅓ cup 2% milk
- 1 tsp. vanilla extract
  Whipped cream or ice cream

1. For sauce, combine brown sugar, cocoa, cornstarch and salt in a large, heavy cast-iron or other ovenproof skillet. Stir in the water; cook, stirring constantly, until mixture begins to boil and thicken slightly. Add butter; mix well. Remove sauce from heat.
2. For dumplings, sift together flour, baking powder, salt, sugar and cocoa. Cut in butter until mixture resembles a fine meal. Combine the egg, milk and vanilla; blend gradually into flour mixture.
3. Return skillet to heat; bring sauce to a boil. Drop dumplings by tablespoonfuls into hot sauce. Reduce heat to low; cover and simmer until just set, about 20 minutes. Serve warm with whipped cream or ice cream.
1 serving: 294 cal., 9g fat (5g sat. fat), 43mg chol., 527mg sod., 52g carb. (33g sugars, 1g fiber), 4g pro.

ALL-TIME CLASSIC

RECIPE INDEX